The 10-Step
Revolution

The 10-Step
Revolution

*RATTLE THE CAGE, IGNITE YOUR
PASSION, AND CREATE YOUR NEW REALITY*

SILVIO GUADAGNINO

SG International Publishing

The 10-Step Revolution

Rattle the cage, Ignite your passion and Create your "New Reality"

Copyright © 2012 by SILVIO GUADAGNINO

All rights reserved

No part of this publication may be reproduced or transmitted in any form or by any means, be it mechanical or electronic, including photocopying and recording, or by any information storage and retrieval system, without permission in writing from Author or Publisher (except by a reviewer, who may quote brief passages and/or show brief video clips in their reviews).

Disclaimer: The Publisher and the Author make no representations or warranties with respect to the accuracy or completeness of the contents of this work and specifically disclaim all warranties, including without limitation warranties of fitness for a particular purpose. No warranty may be created or extended by sales or promotional materials. The advice and strategies contained herein may not be suitable for every situation. This work is sold with the understanding that the Publisher is not engaged in rendering legal, accounting or other professional services. If professional assistance is required, the services of a competent professional person should be sought. Neither the Publisher nor the Author shall be liable for damages arising herefrom. The fact that an organization or website is referred to in this work as a citation and/or a potential source for further information does not mean that the Author or the Publisher endorses the information the organization or website may provide or recommendations it may make. Further, readers should be aware that internet websites listed in this work may have changed or may have disappeared between when this work was written and when it is read.

Published in the United States

ISBN-10: 0988020602

EAN-13: 9780988020603

EAN-13: 9780988020610 (ebook)

Printed in the United States of America

This book is dedicated to every type of revolutionary out there who fought and continues to fight for the causes they believe in until their "New Reality" is established, whether society agrees with them or not.

Lastly, I could not have written this book without special thanks to my wife, family and friends who have endured a lifetime of arguments, screaming and shouting for the causes I supported and continue to support and can finally realize that it all had a purpose.

CONTENTS

Introduction ix

PHASE 1 - REVOLUTION:
(THE "HEADS" SIDE OF THE COIN)

Step 1: 3
If your mind, heart and soul aren't screaming for it...
It's not worthy of a revolution!

Step 2: 11
Revolutions – Nothing more than PMBT!

Step 3: 27
Appeal to the crowd or the revolution is OVER!

Step 4: 43
Don't tight cast the movement

Step 5: 57
Dress rehearsal!

PHASE 2 - ELECTION:
(THE "TALES" SIDE OF THE COIN)

Step 6:   71

Have the "movie script" (I mean draft legal document) ready in advance

Step 7:   91

Negotiation, negotiation and more negotiation!

Step 8:   107

Leverage hard fought battles – It's all in a day's work!

Step 9:   123

The "Schmooze" Factor

Step 10:   137

Race to the polls – Vote to legitimize YOUR revolutionary reform!

Conclusion: 149

The Intangibles

INTRODUCTION

"Energy can neither be created nor destroyed only converted from 1 form to another."

You must be thinking, "Hey, from the title, I thought we were talking about a 10-step guide to creating a revolution that will bring about change; But definitely not a crash course in classical physics" And all I can say is "Don't worry. We are perfectly on track and I'll explain exactly how that is". I'm here to argue that our ability to accomplish the great changes that society and we ourselves so desperately need, come specifically from those individuals who understand how to convert energy from 1 form to another.

Now, despite my engineering background and experience, when I say energy, forget Einstein! What I really mean is how YOU and YOUR GROUP can build momentum for your cause, your vision, ie your REVOLTUION and then convert that energy into a medium that can bring about lasting change and all in a 10-step process of course. A tall order, I know. But before I continue, realize that this 10-step process while clearly applicable to political change is actually applicable to any change from career progression, to environmental to life changes. In the end these are ALL revolutions, be it of different orders of magnitude and flavors but all revolutions nonetheless!

Now, if I was to tell you that you could bring about political change (ie a REVOLUTION – YOUR REVOLUTION) through the machinery of government, your answer would most probably be – ABSOLUTELY…in theory of course. But we all know that in reality that is absolute nonsense. I say this because before you even begin the revolution, the only thing you will see in front of you is the equivalent of Mount Everest and you know what? … It's almost a given that you will quickly surrender! After all in the case of Mount Everest, at least you can actually see most of the perilous terrain – not so for government. So be honest, revolutions, elections environmental change whatever the case may be for you – these are OUR Mount Everest!

At this point, I can say that I understand and empathize with you. In fact the government has become the juggernaut that it is, specifically to crush the little guy and gal into believing deep within their very soul that this powerhouse cannot be toiled with. The only difference here is that this book, my seminars, my speeches, will allow YOU, ME and anyone with the belief in the power of the people and their causes, to rise up and overcome the obstacles standing in the way of your revolution. There is a catch of course; your success stands the best chance of overcoming the obstacles before you if you follow a specific process - the 10-step process explained throughout this book. This blue print of phases and sub steps is of course a fancy way of saying that you have to break up the revolution into parts that are identifiable, that can be completed and then convert the energy from the previous steps at the OPPORTUNE time to an election platform. Then finally convert back to the revolutionary roots to ensure follow through into actual law that legitimizes your actions and sacrifices - Easy right? Maybe not yet, but it will become simpler as you read.

Now the obvious practical application of this step-by-step process is the road to the 2012 elections but it will be equally applicable to the 2016, 2020 election campaigns, as well as the Occupy Wall Street Movement (OWS), your beloved charity movements to your revolution for greater autonomy and advancement in Corporate America. EVERYTHING IN LIFE IS A REVOLUTION, and anytime you request additional salary, a political movement, a shift in foreign policy direction, the election of a new President, you are embarking upon revolutionary change. A change that will be weighed upon by your peers in some form of an "election process" whether you choose to acknowledge this fact or not! Remember, just because the US Presidential election cycle is scheduled, it is still a revolution, a highly organized one at that but still a revolution; after all, the public, if it so chooses, could in theory abstain from the voting process thereby distorting the cycle. It could even legitimize a third party candidate, like Ross Perot in the 1992 campaign. You see the sky is the limit but as you might expect, any revolution is an uphill battle…But not nearly as steep, if you have a 10-step recipe and are always prepared for the next step in the process!

That's right apart from all the propaganda you see on TV, read in books, there is a process, a specific process involved that one must follow to prevail. In many cases the revolutionary's own internal erratic behavior (whether person or group) ends up being the Achilles heel of the revolution, never allowing it to progress to the stage it was meant to achieve – the NEW REALITY; whether that is the implementation of actual law or the acceptance of the new paradigm throughout society!

That's why I titled this book, E-Book, my seminars, coaching and audio materials "The 10-Step Revolution – Rattle the Cage, Ignite your passion, Create your New Reality." I say this because people have to let go of the classical idea of revolutions! That those are once in a life time occurrences that happened during the American Revolution in the 1770's, the civil rights movement of the 1960's, the Sierra Maestra mountains, or the other major cities including London, Rome, Paris, Tokyo and Moscow!

What I intend by the end of this book or through other mediums available to you via www.10steprevolution.com, www.silvioguadagnino.com is for you to realize that only when you treat your idea (ie YOUR CAUSE) as revolutionary, will you begin to summon the power and energy needed to convert that idea into reality. In addition, come to terms with the fact that elections are not processes that simply occur on schedule once every 4 years or at the roar of "No confidence vote"

Introduction

within the chambers of government but every single time you realize that your idea must be weighed and evaluated by a group of your peers locally, nationally and internationally depending on the revolution's magnitude you are about to embark upon!

The best part is, that when you begin to create your revolution, you will have the idea of the link between what I like to refer to as "the two sides of the coin" from the revolution side to the election side – from the "vision" side to the "new reality" side. The energy that fuels the birth or renaissance of any change begins within and burns with the same intensity of a raging forest fire in the California hills but it must be channeled very carefully or it will very quickly fizzle out.

In the end, you must be able to put this currency, this single coin, to work to create the return you long for – True change confirmed and brought to life via a contract or law that can be preserved and defended over time...remind you of anything?... sort of sounds like the recipe of one of the greatest documents ever created.. "The Declaration of Independence" – (After all, if you're going to bring about change – may as well base yourself on one of the best references available)

So, are you now ready to take on your own 10-step-revolution? Are you ready to transform your vision to reality? If you are, grab that coin and let's get started!

Phase 1 Revolution:

(The "heads" side of the coin)

Step 1

if your mind, heart and soul aren't screaming for it...it's not worthy of a revolution!

In this chapter you will learn:
- The mind, heart and soul test
- Time lost / Change gained
- Decision – clerk or soldier/leader of the revolution
- "The Manifesto for Change"

Step 1

if your mind, heart and soul aren't screaming for it...it's not worthy of a revolution!

As the organizer or the initiator of a revolution, you must first prove it to yourself whether the revolution is worth your while! Now this may appear to be an obvious statement, but let me reword it in a more realistic and practical way. If you decide to embark on this incredible journey of change for both you and your cause, you will have little or no time for those other activates that are very important to you and that you might enjoy very much. When I speak of other activities, I mean less time to study for classes during the semester, less time with your girlfriend, boyfriend, wife, husband, less time for sports, shopping or just sitting around watching TV doing nothing. You will have less time to spend with friends that are not involved in the revolution and may even lose some of the friends you currently have. Your life will be infringed upon and beat up by the work load that comes from a serious movement!

Have you ever seen what a true revolutionary looks, sounds and feels like especially in comparison to a joy rider that is simply there for the show! The true revolutionary consciously and subconsciously decided that the movement is part, if not all, of their life! They know more than anything that it takes consistency to shrug off the weight of the status quo and gather momentum for the cause and then keep it going.

I believe that there are points in life when you make decisions, to actually bring about change, but in doing so you have to give up your time and energy so that it can be directed toward the revolution. Let me ask you a question. Is there any idea, point of view that raises your blood pressure to the roof? Is there any one topic that angers the hell out of you? That makes you want to punch a wall! That makes you act, scream, shout and instantaneously jump out of your seat with disgust? For some it's environmental change, for others it's removing or preserving the President in office. In other cases it may be education reform, National Security, or preserving the public's privacy from the government's prying eyes and overreaching forces from such legislation such as the Patriots Act. Regardless, of your situation, it must have that feeling as the launching point for your work. If it does not I can simply say one thing! Get out now and don't waste your time!

I know, all the purists must be screaming out now especially since the entire grass roots movement in politics is based on the premise of getting voter turnout to the ballot boxes for example; but remember you are embarking on your own revolution, or one that may have been started by others and that is most probably at odds with strong government forces and so you must truly believe in the cause. It must be as true to you as the march for civil rights or the Gospel shouted out by a priest or minister at Sunday mass and if it doesn't move you in that way, you must decide on the following before continuing,

Am I a clerk of the movement or
a soldier/leader of the revolution?

Be honest with yourself! Are you going to be the kind of person that will help sending email and fliers once a week on Saturday afternoon or the person who's schedule contains daily, weekly and monthly tasks linked directly to the goals and master blue print for the revolution?.

The idea here is to instill in you the reality of the situation; the fact that you will be singled out and discriminated against for your beliefs. Do you think that the environmental movement was embraced at the beginning? By the way, it still isn't in most circles but thanks to public pressure, companies and industries must tread lightly in these murky waters, pardon the pun!

Now all this is NOT to discourage you into giving up on your cause! In fact, it's quite the opposite. I want you to be prepared for the work ahead with the additional incentive, actually an added assurance in knowing that you will have a plan, a 10-step process to guide and help you on your way to great change. I believe my process can help you achieve your final goal but the outcome really depends on YOU!

One more thing, "don't worry about all the little things you'll miss along the way!" The beauty of revolutions is that you get to see society through a different lens. One that filters through all of the useless that we call life. Ask anyone who took part in the 1960s black rights movement, the environmental fight, and Occupy Wall Street (OWS) Revolution taking place at this very moment! These movements made or are making history and let me include a disclaimer right now! Not all of them will come to fruition but being part of something life altering not only changes society…It changes YOU! And usually for the better!

What I want to know is whether, you feel, and believe that you can give your heart, your soul and most importantly, contrary to popular belief anyways, YOUR MIND, to the revolution. You MUST give all 3 right now, or take your place outside or at most as a clerk in the revolution! Throughout my life, I have always been one to believe in a cause, always protect and defend the ideas I hold dear regardless of where I find myself. It's exactly for this reason I write my books, give speeches and seminars. Who knows we may even be on the same side of many issues and find ourselves fighting injustices together?

With all this talk of heart, soul and mind, there might be some confusion and fear that the information here is only general. Don't be! We are going to get very hands on right now. I would like for you to go to my website www.silvioguadagnino.com right now and fill out the form I call "The Manifesto for Change" only now we are going to verbalize and explain what it is YOU are really after! This exercise is incredible. It somehow has the disarming effect of displaying all of the holes and lack thereof in your argument. Even more importantly I want you to explain in no more than 2 sentences what you want to accomplish and how it would appear in society after the revolution and corresponding election you helped plan and launch were implemented into law! Next I want you to estimate the amount of time you think it will take to actually get this done.

Are you done? Of course not; it might take a while! – it has taken a life time in some cases – But I'll tell you one thing – what you really want, whether you want to believe it or not is usually already known to you – you just probably never took the time to look! So when you're done, step aside and take that timeline and split it in two, one side for the revolution to take place and the other for its conversion to an election schedule. Of course some activities from the 2 phases can and will overlap. You see after this extremely simple but subtle exercise, you will actually have the backbone for your revolution – Aren't you happy you gave up some of your time to prove to yourself what you were thinking and feeling was actually real?

Step 2

Revolutions - Nothing more than PMBT!

In this chapter you will learn:

- How good are you at marketing? Seriously!
- Exercise 1 – Three bullet points
- Exercise 2 – Write down everything important you can think of – mold it into a Business Case
- The next mistake future revolutionaries make is to think that companies and governments don't care about people. They actually DO... But indirectly.
- The Sales pitch battling it out against the Business Case
- Your pitch must have an angle to attract people despite all the interference and distraction that society offers.

that fit seamlessly in their day-to-day life all the while helping your organization achieve its goal for minimizing waste in your community. The list goes on and on. After you are done with this introspection, you must summarize this information to complete this part of the exercise 2. This part of the exercise is usually overlooked because people do not associate revolutions with it, but without it you have no foundation for one. Are you enjoying the buildup? – there's practically a drum roll in the background – Basically you need to take the information summarized above and use it to create your Business Case for the revolution. All of your actions whether from the vision/revolutionary side to the electoral/"New reality" side of the coin will have to be guided and tagged to some part of this business case to help provide direction to the revolution. This is absolutely required because ultimately whether you choose to accept it or not, you will have to show evidence that your revolution makes "financial sense" to the government entity or corporation you are trying to overcome or convince. This is the point most people forget. For different templates of business cases refer to my website www.silvioguadagnino.com.

The next error future revolutionaries make is to think that companies and governments don't care about people. They actually do…but indirectly! Let me explain. What these entities really care about is the continuation of society, about ensuring that its economic wheels are greased so that we continue to chug along as expected. You see government doesn't like change because change is a gamble that can go terribly wrong! It can quickly deplete the Treasury's coffers and intern result in an increase in taxes. Believe it or not, the Iraq war (read about the strategies for war in my first book "The Means to a Chosen End" www.chosenend.com) was a revolution whether the government chooses to call it such or not! It was the government's decision, to occupy/control a foreign land to ensure the steady flow of precious cargo (oil), to American shores as required by our economy to sustain our way of life. Whether you choose to agree with the Bush/Obama Administration or not, it boils down to a choice that they felt was worth taking; a choice to maintain the requirements demanded by the industrial complex. In other words this "revolution" had a viable business case, and was a choice explained to the American people through nothing more than a Sales Pitches tweaked for the audience in attendance at that very moment. The other major sub-factor to consider in any business case is the timeline. A variable that should always be capped but was purposely maintained without limits for obvious military reasons in this case. The problem that occurs when you do not attribute a date of completion to this or any task for that matter, is that a much greater cost will have to be paid than was initially expected, without any assurance for victory! In the case of the Iraq/Afghan war, the miscalculation amounted to thousands of American casualties, a huge financial cost to taxpayers via the increase in public debt, the instability in the region and the list goes on and on.

You see this revolution just as in any other, has the Sales pitch battling it out against the Business

Case and as you might imagine, however noble the revolution, the sales pitch will lose the fight if the business case isn't rock solid. No sales pitch, however convincing, can possibly overtake the immense financial costs associated with a flawed business case such as a war without a preconceived exit plan in case of failure or the incalculable social effect of losing thousands of soldiers whose pain and suffering is without financial equivalent. In the end the vision/ revolution and eventual corresponding election/ new reality, boils down to a fascinating and dangerous game of tug-of-war between a sales pitch and a business case!

I think this would be the perfect opportunity to provide an example everyone can understand. Take the Presidential campaign of 2012 or the prior campaign of 2008 or any other past and future campaign for that matter, and these are all revolutions; controlled yes, but they are still revolutions. This is a strange fact I know, because we tend to not think of them in this light but that is exactly what they are! The 2008 campaign was responsible for electing the first African American President to the highest office in the land. In the 1960's they couldn't even use the same bathrooms as white people! – now there's a revolution if I have ever seen one and it, just like all the others was based on an elegant sales pitch for change coupled with a mission statement/business case with strict deadlines to gage its success. Regardless of the magnitude, if you don't have these 4 factors understood and accounted for don't even waste your time. You may be thinking that this might be the case in politics but what about other situations, as many would argue that outside the epicenter of the revolution the emotional impact diminishes greatly among the general public; a logical argument. So take the environmental movement fighting to save pandas from going extinct. Now perhaps the WWF World Wildlife Foundation may be screaming about the extinction of pandas in China but in all honesty, the majority of people on the streets really don't care. And how could they, since they have to worry about paying their mortgages or being foreclosed on. I have even noticed that many people today are simply faking it just to avoid being scolded by society for their "lack of morals".

You see, in this second example, much more removed from everyday life than the first, you quickly realize that this case demands that your sales pitch have a very pointed angle to attract people who would otherwise tune out due to all the interference, distortion and distraction that society offers. And that is a tall order. Now imagine, just for a minute that instead of pandas I said that cows, if not taken care of could go instinct - without even mentioning a deadline! Crazy I know, but just imagine how different this would be received. Once explained that they would no longer be able to enjoy a juicy steak, cheese, or fresh glass of milk in the morning for them or their children, they would surely rise to the occasion. They would never let such a situation continue to decline. Do you see the difference between this case and that of the pandas? In the panda case pitch and timeline are absolutely essential because if I was to say pandas would go extinct in 150 years I personally would not give it another thought and neither would 90% of the people whereas in the hypothetical case for cows, action would be taken immediately without even the slightest mention of time.

The reason, I brought up this comparative example between cows and pandas, is simple. Most people will not listen to any message regardless of its importance unless it's backed by all 4 factors including the concise sales pitch, mission statement/business case and timeline! Even then, if the sales pitch doesn't explain and convince them why this particular issue outranks the millions of others in their lives they will not feel the pressure and gravity of the situation required for them to take action and you will intern have waited your time

Now once you have a concise description of the revolution including the PMBT and its relative ranking of importance, here is your chance to pump it up with steroids. This is of course completely independent of the livestock discussion from the previous paragraphs earlier of course!

This part I believe is where the real energy of those infused by the idea can truly shine! You see the idea of informing and propagating a revolution over the internet and social media facilitates the logistics and communication process immensely but you must remember that these social sites are the medium not the actual message. Your words, ideas and most importantly actions, are the message that must be seen, heard and felt by the public at large or the revolution will remain an abstract concept instead of the real life solution to a problem that will affect and change their lives.

Furthermore, the beauty of these public moments is that they allow you to be theatrical allowing people to judge in a single instant, whether they identify with the movement or not. But be careful and remember that even if you have hundreds of thousands of followers on YouTube or Face Book, if you are not able to gather protestors to rally in the streets for the cause, these climactic moments, or the lack thereof, may be the beginning of the end for your revolution.

Next, does the timeline actually make sense… with your schedule? Especially if you're starting the revolution from scratch; if the revolution is already in motion, analyze the PMBT – the lack of one is red flag for failure.

In this day and age, it is very probable that you are embarking upon a revolution that already exists which is good in one way as much of the logistics may already be in place including a list of supporters and volunteers that simply need to be revived. In these cases before you do anything else, it is your job to review all of the literature that exists so that you can take the helm quickly and effortlessly; but regardless of the head start you must first review and most probably update the PMBT for the revolution so that it becomes yours and not a rerun of those from earlier years and past generations.

Perhaps the most important lesson of all regarding past progress is right before your very eyes; if you choose to pay attention. The beauty of taking on a dormant revolution is that you just received a sneak peak at what happens to energy when not directed through the proper channels. When you don't follow a regimented plan that allows for flexibility like the one outlined in this book, it becomes highly probable that you will fail. Furthermore, your research will quickly provide a snap shot of the organizational structure or in many cases, the lack there of. You can see whether the previous group had any kind of marketing campaign or whether they were simply blowing hot air. If they did have some kind of sales pitch it may be evidence that that type of a campaign may not have been the right approach at the time.

This information should then be overlapped to any further blue prints you can retrieve from organizations in other communities or those involved at the state or national level. Furthermore, they may already have all of these necessary PMBT documents generalized across multiple campaigns that simply need to be tailored to your community. Be careful though, as any time spent working on preexistent documents will actually amount to time wasted that could otherwise have been allocated towards the creation of a campaign central in your community, recruiting, raising funds etc. This would allow you to channel your energy properly and is perhaps most important in election campaigns, because ideally if every community had a center of operations, information regarding polling and voter reactions, could allow campaigns the ability to understand and win elections 1 community at a time.

This is also the time to analyze in great detail the aspirations of the organization or small group. In the case of a startup it is the time to fine-tune the arguments that make people tick, the arguments that enrage, inspire and fuel their actions that create the waves required to make change a reality. So get to work maestro!

Now you're ready to create/modify the Sales Pitch. A daunting task I know! "But wait a second, isn't that something high powered Cola executives do for a living?" – Don't worry; and don't be scared to ask for professional help

Before we continue, I have a question for you; if you were working on a new project or starting a new job, wouldn't you begin your first day by discussing the tasks and the project with a colleague or in the case of current employment perhaps discuss the changes that can be implemented with a consultant to jumpstart or reenergize a sagging or deteriorating situation? These are definitely all very probable situations and the same idea is true for your Sales Pitch, Business Case, Mission Statement and timeline.

If you agree with the idea above why not take your ideas to a marketing firm that can revamp the strategy into one Mainstream America can accept and help implement through their purchasing power. Remember, these marketing guys will find the best angles without being partial or emotional. The best part is if they do hit the bull's eye with regards to the right campaign slogan or emblem, with your knowledge and experience you will be able to notice it almost instantaneously.

I know that there may be those who are screaming uncontrollably after mentioning Marketing firms since they simply may not have the money to pay big shot firms to help with the campaign! To those readers all I can say is – current college/university grads and undergrads looking for real life projects to hone their skills. Who knows, you may get the opportunity to meet a future marketing heavy weight that will be working on your campaign for free!

I believe the beauty of a revolution, especially one that starts from scratch, is that you are the very heart beat of the revolution. It's exciting. I remember writing my first book "The Means to a Chosen End" available on www.amazon.com or go to www.silvioguadagnino.com and feeling absolutely alive and full of energy as I proposed that the war in Iraq/Afghanistan was dependent on a dozen or so variables and that if manipulated properly, the ideas would allow the reader to come to his or her own decision regarding the US's position on the war. This idea excited me and all those I spoke to because the plan filtered through all the noise in society letting the reader truly decide for themselves and then be able to defend their decision from those opposing them regardless of whether they were for or against. That is what I mean by revolution. It begins with inspiration, the willingness to tackle big or small issues regardless of the counter arguments proposed by others and providing an actual step-by-step process to allow the reader, future activist to decide and hopefully join the revolution so that it can take shape and eventually change society!

The best part about the whole process was that I realized that the ideas I wrote about for Iraq are equally applicable in other settings which never dawned on me initially. That's what I mean when I say you learn new things and keep learning long afterwards.

Lastly, remember you may be the face of the revolution – but you must have a structure and lieutenants to succeed you if need be such that the revolution endures.

If it turns out that you are the face of the revolution or perhaps carrying the torch of the former revolutionary, your first task is to reinstitute a structure for the new "edition" of the revolution you're heading. But in spite of all your work and good intention realize that in most cases the revolution may not end with you. You may be the initiator, the follow through man/woman or simply one of the many profits for the cause, so whatever you do, do not become one of the long line of self destructive leaders society has become so accustomed to. In other words, do not become "corrupted" by the power of your position. After all, if you truly are a great leader, your followers will be pleading with you to stay should you ever choose to leave! I guess this is the simplest but one of the most difficult ideas to digest especially when you were part of or were the one that created the PMBT that got the ball rolling! So beware of others who may be tempted by a revolution's attraction and most of all of ourselves as we somehow are most surprised by our own actions and desires for the power to control something that began with the greatest of intentions!

Ultimately, you may be at the center of the revolution (for now) – but you are NOT the revolution and it must continue whether you are part of it or not! Never forget this and you'll make a great leader.

Step 3

Appeal to the crowd or the revolution is OVER!

In this chapter you will learn:

- The revolution must encompass certain ideas dormant in the public that when arisen create a wave of energy and anger in the crowds

- The crowds must be guided to a final stance; whether they know it or not!

- The crowd is really a bunch of groups – be sure not to put them at odds with one another – remember to divide and conquer the enemy not your troops (or in this case activists/supporters)

- Your message will become more poignant and sharp with more and more speeches

- Make the crowd wait and scream for you – there's no difference between a crowd at a concert and one at political rally – the same rules apply
- Once you have the belief of the masses – the revolution can then take flight

Step 3

Appeal to the crowd or the revolution is OVER!

Most revolutions tend to go through cycles, peaks and troughs usually ending up dormant until the cycle is reinvigorated and dies out yet again. Why is it that the most important issues of our lives and by extension those of society tend to fade away so easily? Isn't your privacy, the environment, the cost of an education important to you? What would it take to jumpstart your revolution? To raise it from the dead and recapture the interest and vibrancy it once possessed.

I believe that this see-saw effect has everything to do with the Roman Coliseum! ...Yes the Roman Coliseum! You must be thinking, "There he goes again, completely off track but it's usually for a reason – I hope!" Don't worry, what I mean is, your movement, if it is to be successful must have all the elements required to entertain the crowd while being informative and instructive. Your revolution must be able to divert attention elsewhere when needed as well as be a place where people can discuss issues, shout out their grievances, be mean and say all the things they feel whether the government agrees with them or not. You see, energy feeds on itself but if there is none to begin with how can it possibly be converted to something meaningful?

In keeping with my earlier statement, if I asked you to describe the Coliseum, the first ideas that probably come to mind would be the roar of the crowd, the fierceness of the life or death battle on the arena's center stage; the ability for the crowd to elevate one of the gladiators to a height of fury that would allow him the power and adrenaline to overcome his opponent leading to blood-stained sand along the arena floor and of course the mixing of all facets of society, from the commoners, to senators all the way up to the emperor himself! All that makes perfect sense right but what you haven't realized is that in the stands are regular everyday people discussing life at length despite all the carnage. People just like you and I talking about what they both admire and despise about the society we live in.

They would be talking about the possibility of Rome advancing her territories in Eastern Europe or the bill before senate for the inclusion of a new tax that would apply to all of Roman Society. Perhaps, talk of the creation of a new temple, like the Pantheon or the continuation of the Roman roads linking the empire to all of its lands allowing for greater communication. I don't know about you but it sounds a lot like Washington or any modern day city including Rome in the present day. As you can see, it is crucial for a revolution to appeal to the crowds to allow for downtime but at the same time provide a way for the people, whether they agree or not with all the points of the movement to be together and feel as one. Do you have a place like this? Perhaps the basement of your home where the revolution began or a public library or a bar where you can discuss the ideas over drinks; Regardless you need a place to meet, discuss, plan and manage your revolution – you need a war room you need your own "Coliseum".

I also believe that the passage of time is in fact our greatest enemy. Despite the firm belief in the revolutionary idea being pursued, every challenge within a society, however small or large, tends to be engulfed in turmoil and descent from within. The sad fact is that opponents usually overcome most revolutions by simply letting it run its course and fizzle away. You see most of the time it's not the government that destroys the movement, it's an implosion from within - it's the people themselves. The subgroups within the organization fight amongst themselves to the point where they simply hate their ally and either quit or break away into a smaller groups, which of course makes the revolution that much weaker and your opponent that much happier!

So what do you suppose I'm proposing after sliding you along this tangent of history? Well, it's quite simple! You must always ensure that you appeal to your crowd! That you keep them entertained with the spectacles of the day, whether its sports or movies, great books etc but regardless of your strategy you must appeal to all or as many facets of your crowd as possible. What people may not realize is that if you give a great speech for example, some of the hard core political enthusiast will decide to join the ranks, but for those who are not, or those considered the equivalent of seasonal window shoppers, you most probably turned them off or at best only temporarily caught their attention. But if you start to have get-togethers with the group for an activity that appeals to them, then they will begin to see you in another light. All of a sudden you become real; a person they want to be around, and most importantly a person they admire and want to emulate! And then when they finally understand, and realize that you are one of them then you may be able to convince them ending up with true supporters! So start small and people will come!

Apart from keeping the people occupied there is another factor that cannot be denied – VISUAL APPEAL! I hate to say this since in theory content should win over medium but most of the time you win the people over and keep them by your side simply by the way you look, act, approach and talk with them. And in theory this really has nothing to do with the actual revolution. A leader must encompass everything the crowd represents and the one who is most well rounded tends to lead. Think about it, even in high school, who tended to win the elections? The most popular guy in school that everyone liked and wanted to be; He didn't know everything, but he knew everyone that could provide him with the information he needed as well as the organizers to ensure the turnout for the win. Do you really think that your revolution would be exempt from such primitive and natural influences? It isn't and so you must always keep this point in mind. In the end the Coliseum had nothing to do with the Roman Senate but what a great place to gage the pulse of the people while disarming them with the show!

I feel that this point must be hammered into people's mind because if you take away all the poetry surrounding a revolution, all of the eloquence and national anthems, the documents and laws set forward, a revolution is nothing more than a crowd moving together as one despite the multitude of forces trying to hold it back! That's all it really is, so don't be fooled! Even more importantly realize that amongst the crowd are people with completely different points of view who have decided that this idea outweighs even their stiffest counter argument.

Take OWS for example. The "crowd" in this movement appears at first glance to be quite diversified but when you begin to scratch the surface you realize that despite the broad interest it is quite shallow. I say this because you as a revolutionary must distinguish between those people who sympathize with the movement coming from all walks of life and the actual "soldiers" on the street who are mainly young college student and grads that are out of work and blame the establishment. So my question to you is, "do you think that that the Wall Street movement is appealing to the crowds or not?"

Now I will probably be criticized for saying this but I believe that the movement is limited to a select group and that while it appears to have a large scale following, in reality is mainly confined to a small percentage of the entire population! Let me ask you, do you think anyone over 55 will believe in this cause, perhaps in theory and in some abstract way yes, but as an actual protestor, absolutely not! Right there is about 20% of the population that is indifferent, not to mention all of those people that are employed, happy, and/or satisfied or at least grateful for their current job. These people will also not be enticed by this movement. Furthermore, Corporate America and its employees will certainly oppose such a movement as well as anyone working for a government agency well compensated by the state. So what you have in the end is a monolithic group that people in high places look down upon. Now despite the resistance, or indifference which is just as toxic, from those in power, I must reiterate that these reactions from the outside are not the problem because these can be overcome.

The real problem in this case is that the Occupy Wall Street movement has not been able to find its voice with the many crowds because at this point in time anyway, it is not appealing to the general public. It's only appealing to a certain group of people and completely ignoring others. In actuality, you are only able to see the cracks once you take a step back and realize that the crowds "somehow sense" that they don't have a serious sales pitch. The pitch is drenched in generality dripping with ideas of greed and the allocation of power in society. These generalities and refusal to acknowledge the fact that the nation has been a capitalist society since its inception are its downfall. Furthermore, there's no timeline and certainly no business case set forward and so you are almost guaranteed that such a movement will simply die out due to its lack of a well defined purpose and loss of interest amongst a single minded crowd

Now, I know some might argue that their strength lies in the fact that they can create a protest in any city around the world and that unlike the Wikileak's phenomena, it can't be stopped as there really is no leader to guillotine! These are very good points by the way, with which I do agree, but the underlying fact remains; the movement is without a head, pardon the pun, and as such it will die due to a lack of direction. And the worst part is that the majority of people are already beginning to agree with governments that these same protestors are overstaying their welcome and have fallen out of favor with the general public. You see right there, I can say that this movement has lost yet another section of the crowd, not because it doesn't have a platform but because it does not have a mechanism to create a community for all participants. And most of all it would not be able to convert such weak arguments to an actual election question on a ballot and as such its life is limited.

Please note that all of my arguments above, in particular the notion of treating this or any movement simply as a group of crowds that must be directed has been ignored by this movement. I am in my early thirties, working in the corporate world, and I can tell you that people my age are not "occupied" with this movement at all! And you know why? Because the message to the mainstream has not been propagated to the different groups within the crowd as it should be! They have literally ignored this crucial part of the population. The population (ie crowd) that actually works! And simply from a numbers standpoint, this "crowd" is the most important.

So instead of rambling on, we must now get to work at a specific tactic I call "Bases Covered". What you need to realize is that your revolution and its sales pitch never change, if fact they shouldn't unless there is a major shift in the doctrine of the revolution. On the other hand if you want to be able to convince both the 22-year-old unemployed college grad as well as the 50 year old seasoned blue collar employee, you will definitely need to customize the message to ensure that you are making it worth their while to give you their time and energy and ultimately their vote when it gets to that stage.

The best part is, that since you are most probably not part of the government your mission is single minded and as such has the possibility for success further increases.

Guide the people to their final decision via your arguments and actions always using their energy against them. In most cases people actually know that the revolution is just but they are not convinced. So it is your job to divert and for the lack of more appropriate words, force them into action. I say force because they actually already made the decision subconsciously when they showed up at the meetings in the first place.

The process works like clockwork. A person is attracted by the idea of a revolution; they learn about it and are attracted to it despite the fact that they may not even be able to explain their reasoning. They take time out of their day to show up at a rally and there lies the point of no return. You see once they are there, they feel a kinship with the person next to them; As though they understand each other. At this point the work is pretty much done. Now is your opportunity as leader to take individuals infused with emotion and leverage the power of numbers to guide them on their next task towards victory.

It is at this crucial point in time that you must provide the crowd, including all its subgroups, with both the grandeur of the long term plan as well as the short term goals that links into the master plan. You are in many ways manipulating them but in their own best interests and to achieve a common goal. With this in mind here is an exercise that will get you headed in the right direction.

Exercise: If you were heading the next Occupy Wall Street protest in your town or city what would your speech include?

What you must realize is that if you don't have that kind of speech ready along with contingency plans depending on what the local authorities throw at you, your protest is the equivalent of a fight between a 5 year old kid and parents scolding him for not doing his homework!

Throughout this book I will continually ask that you complete exercises. These will make you think and realize that revolutions really are chess matches and the government while big and strong, lack the mobility and belief that a well organized group possess.

Furthermore, this isn't a "1960s flower power" protest against a war in a foreign land; now people are taking on capitalism at home, - the big banks, immigration, budget cuts, environmental reform all threatening your very way of life and the pocket books of each and every person, especially of those in power. These changes make any war seem like a joke since wars in faraway lands are extremely simple to demonize. Whereas the actions of certain banks or political parties probably garner as much support as they do opposition by the people at large.

The idea here is to present a case to your people with cause/effect scenarios but ensure that prior to every encounter with the "enemy" you have stepped into their shoes to understand how he or she would respond. Go to the length of actually enacting and taking on your enemy's body! Just remember to come back of course! The beauty of this exercise is that you really do realize however distorted the counter argument, that that person has a goal in mind. And if you intend to achieve your goal you must provide something to him that will make him question himself, fold and ultimately surrender. But, the best way to reach a mutual decision is to ensure that the final law provides concessions for both parties. If only one party's demands are completely satisfied then you can expect the treaty, business deal, compromise to erode as there would be no balance for the other side. In the case of Germany after World War I for example, the heavy debt and inflation burden painted the scene for World War II whether the average Joe chooses to accept this idea or not. This was a case where the victors had the right to force the Germans to pay for losses but without balance as explained earlier, it simply paved the way to a second world war.

Within any group there are subgroups that receive more attention and that by their very internal energy propel it forward to the dismay of all those involved. If you look at the Republican Party, the party of Lincoln, it is currently divided into a hard core conservative wing, a Tea Party establishment, along with a majority right of center view. Despite the ability for the Democrats and Republicans to discuss and pass laws in the past, that ability to compromise has completely melted away. The same idea holds true on the Democrats front but to a lesser a degree.

It is absolutely essential for any revolution that you as the leader/organizer must ensure that these kind of internal subgroups are discouraged. That at the very instant that such sub organizations begin to present themselves, you as a leader must take action? But what would or could you do? There are a few ideas but perhaps the first step would be to ensure that people from opposite sides are brought together to discuss their philosophical differences all the while working together towards the same goal.

Do this by having debates internally so that you can note, understand and prepare all the counter arguments that will probably be proposed by your real opponent from the outside. Realize that this internal struggle does not hurt the revolution; it actually makes it stronger, if and only if it is addressed immediately and internally. Discuss how these ideas could be included in the Business Case, Mission Statement and thereby translated into the Sales Pitch for the revolution.

In addition, when struggle occurs internally, reaffirm to those lashing out that within your circle you can all work together to create common goals but if you were to go to the outside, others would use these difficulties and weak spots to destroy the revolution as a hole. This tactic has the added benefit of exposing those individuals and subgroups that are more interested in their own personal beliefs than those of the cause. Basically as leader, the ability to gage and limit descent is one of the tell-tale signs of great leadership.

Lastly, after all your work, judge for yourself and then as a group whether you believe that the breakaway sect is worth working with or whether it should simply break away since in many cases those very internal arguments consume more energy than those from the outside.

As you begin to make the rounds in speeches and small group discussions, slowly and without warning you will realize that your message is continually being fine tuned via reactions to your words and actions. This feedback from the crowds is amongst the most important, but only if you get into the habit of logging all that you learn as soon as you receive it. What I mean is, if your arguments tend to receive praise consistently throughout your discussions in the community or state, your log will have confirmed it. The same goes for weak arguments that appear to lack clarity for the people. Note their reactions in great detail, both physical and verbal. See how simple or difficult it is to get them to understand and accept your point of view. If they ever do at all! Recruit those in the audience that demonstrate the fire and intelligence needed by the cause. See how you should thread together the different arguments to ensure that the proper flow exists and that the speech is digestible to those in attendance.

Also, after every speech always ask those in attendance what they feel could be added, removed and elaborated upon. These people may even introduce you to ideas you never even considered!

Just as importantly, see how your public speaking skills rate after a few speeches and throughout your campaign; turns out that sometimes, certain people are better researchers than orators and you may have to make a choice to either learn to fine-tune the tricks of the trade or let someone else take on the pulpit! Finally remember that in the case of political speeches.

The truth of the matter is that there really is no difference between a crowd at a concert and one at a political rally. The exact same rules apply; from the orators control over the crowd, to their command of the peaks, troughs, tone and speed of the words spoken. Then when he/she adds a coat of body language and the warmth of his or her voice to the affair - a star is born! Better than that, a man or woman of the people. Only this kind of star can really change the world!

Step 4

Don't tight cast the movement

In this chapter you will learn:

- Anyone and everyone should be part of your movement – the revolution needs messengers of all shapes and sizes and colors
- Have a lead for each group that reports to you to ensure that the message is based on the mission statement and tailored to the group
- Don't see corporate America as the enemy – to do so is to kill the movement before it ever starts
- Short sightedness could destroy the plan
- Your town, borough, district, riding is the grass roots experiment – the national scene is exactly the same but magnified

- Lastly, there will most probably be groups in the community that disagree – no problem, just continually keep track of their percentage of the general population

Step 4

Don't tight cast the movement

Before you generalize and think that a movement is at its heart shared by a single group, be advised that you are on track to defeat! What you need to keep in mind is that revolutions must be understood and supported on as many fronts as possible. The possibility to enlist the abilities and knowledge of as many groups as possible is key to the sustainment of a cause.

Say I was to tell you that the youth in the US are rallying support around the country for a cause such as Education reform, what would you say? My first response would be, "yeah, tell me something I don't know!" since this reaction is an ongoing theme that never gains any political traction. I think it's because once you graduated and are loaded with debt, isn't there a part of you, however small, that believes that since I had to go through it and am now constrained by the debt loads, why shouldn't the next guy feel the same way and step into the same shoes. This is precisely the kind of thought process that I believe takes place, simply because it is human nature to do so. What you as the reader and activist need to realize is that if education reform protests affected more than just a single age group, but actually spread out over many sections of the population, perhaps those cries would actually gain some traction.

Say for example, that instead of a rally being filled with only students, that you got your parents and seniors to accompany you at these rallies? What would happen to the dynamics of the whole protest? Well firstly, it would take on added exposure, added acceptance by the media establishment, and most importantly the realization by congress that the issue now has infiltrated many of the macro communities within society! The truth is, people in power don't care about college students but not because they are heartless, after all they once were in your very shoes, but simply because they have too many other problems on their hands! There are possible wars, financial meltdowns, debt and deficits that make the numbers look like they were calculated by people on illegal substances. Do you really believe they will stop to take on an issue like this! The important idea to take away is that this revolution, just like any other, is guilty of the most common error of humankind – in fact one of its greatest deficiencies; people innately tend to ally themselves with someone who is as close a match to them as possible; physically, intellectually, spiritually and financially. Why do you think that the Occupy Wall Street protestors all look the same regardless of the country or city they take place. What people are missing in these rallies are representation by all segments of the community with the numbers and speakers to explain why this particular revolution is a matter that affects them personally and their respective group. Now, imagine for a second that these protestors (ie the revolution) were thinking 5 steps ahead; if this was the case they would plan with the flip side of the coin in mind. I am of course referencing my earlier analogy but the idea being that the ultimate goal is the conversion of the idea into a Bill that can be enacted into law. Now if the protestors had this idea in mind, they would equally have to realize that this can only be accomplished by attracting all segments of the population to their rallies because whether protestors choose to believe it or not, at the end of the day, your work is simply a waist of your time unless you brought about change affirmed through the creation of law. But you can't achieve this goal unless you have the manpower throughout society pushing, dare I say harassing, their elected officials to act.

Imagine for a moment being the Congressman of your district with protests by college students taking place throughout the year. Imagine that you are looking out to them and speaking with the crowds at town halls. What would you think looking into the crowd? I'll tell you what both you and they would think if you were in those shoes, "looks like a sea of student voters, that I have to sympathize with, but given the general student habits, they probably are occupied with projects and exams after which dating, sex, drugs take their ever clamping hold on the individual; then what's left a few students that march their way down a campus and feel as though they had their "60s protest moment"...and then it'll be over; repeating itself once again with next years' graduating class." That's what I believe really goes on in the minds of congressmen and women.

Now imagine if every student would ask a parent, uncle or aunt, a cousin all of which are part of the working and taxpaying class to accompany their rallies. What would happen? Firstly, the number of people would swell up to an uncomfortable number that would make any police force worry at the security risks. It would create the feeling that this idea is NOW extending beyond the campus limits to those in "real" life. Even more importantly, that congressman is now thinking twice about what he might say or how he'll react because NOW the movement is no longer tight cast to a select crowd, but is spreading like wild fire to all the different facets of society! These are the kind of changes in society that make those in charge say, "wait a second, this issue is bigger and more dangerous than we thought".

That same group of protestors should then plan the subsequent rallies not along the university lawns but around city hall or the state legislature at scheduled and unscheduled points in time. As you might expect the government and the establishment doesn't like surprise, nor do they like the idea of a people sticking together.

Now just imagine if those same students aided by their parents and grandparents for tuition reform then showed up at a rally for senior's medical expenses reform? What would result is truly revolutionary – if this was to take place this phenomenon would force lawmaker far and wide, to act as demanded by their constituents or suffer the consequences come election time. What you have is one movement fueling the other with the combined energy and momentum of both camps! Can you start to feel the energy of this kind of momentum; the heat from this kind of wild fire especially once this partnership really starts to catch on? Strangely enough, this kind of energy and its channeling in a given direction doesn't take rocket science but it must overcome the notion of tight casting and the acceptance of intermingling of powerful groups in society that would otherwise remain diametrically opposed or completely independent of one another!

I have always believed and continue to believe that society can only be strong when we join forces. That was and is the way all countries are formed. Do you truly believe that the United States could have been formed without the acceptance by every single facet of the population? Absolutely not, and so why would you think education reform, preventative wars or Medicare would be any different!

Why not on Saturday? – the flip side of the coin: There are so many examples of "united protests that you can plan including a rally at city hall or the state legislature on Saturday morning with your parents!" I know, all of a sudden the whole idea of the protest movement seems a lot less glamorous right? But on the other hand so much more effective since society and its disagreement with the establishment will have been voiced by a large segment of the population. Perhaps, flooding the annual Macy's Thanksgiving Day parade with banners along the entire route proclaiming the infamous Sales Pitch (ie slogan) for the entire country to see and question at the expense of the mainstream media. You could potentially have brought those same flash cards to an NFL football game and wave them throughout the broadcast. Perhaps you could show up in New York where one of the many morning shows film live outside, and grab the attention of a live audience. Basically, people need to realize that there is a platform everywhere you look, but you simply need to take the action needed and build a multi-faceted campaign.

Now that you have come to term with the lack of awareness and the inherent discriminatory ways of the majority of revolutions, it would be best to provide visibility to these newly appointed powerful internal lobby group managers and assign responsibilities for their recruiting of future members. Furthermore, if you want to get all the groups to add to the power of the revolution each group must have a seat at the table to discuss the strategy and content of the movement to ensure that all messages go out with a single voice and purpose.

If I was running the Occupy Wall Street movement, I would do everything possible to ensure that there was a member representing as many of the respective groups as possible in that particular city, but despite this fact when I look at the OWS movement in its current form I must admit it does have a distinct nimbleness about it! For one thing, there is no clear cut leader as was the case with Wikileaks which makes it more difficult to cut off the head of the movement! Also, OWS's ability to address different problems directly related to that particular city is unquestionably a powerful weapon at their disposal. In that sense my opinion in assigning a head for each group with a leader for each OWS city does appear to be old fashioned, top heavy and very easy to infiltrate by those dead set on diffusing its power and appeal. But regardless of these pros and cons, this current loosely-fit OWS network version will ultimately fall apart! They always do and in this case let's be honest, they are taking on "crony capitalism" as it's sometimes referred to. I personally disagree with this idea of crony because part of me knows that the only reason we have food on the table at relatively low prices, with inflation being the rampant enemy of course, is because of capitalism. Do you honestly think you could have bananas in Cleveland in the dead of winter if it wasn't for this network diminishing the costs as much as possible? On the other hand, those same people who despise capitalism will pay 6$ to 8$ for a latte when you could have it at a no name café or McDonalds for about 1.50$. Perhaps some clarification is required for the distinction between capitalism and marketing that subconsciously makes us make choices we would otherwise never come to ourselves. Lastly, I didn't see that many people complaining when they saw their real estate values increasing throughout the

2004 to 2007 height. Take a look prior to 2008, not many OWS rallies huh? I think capitalism depends on which side your on at that very moment, and it is precisely for this reason that the OWS movement, Presidential Election campaigns must take the time and effort to view the situation from the so-called "enemy's" point of view. Better yet speak with some of the so-called "enemies" directly to develop ideas and strategies as to how the system can be adjusted through the implementation of specific rules. In keeping with the ideas mentioned above, all these different types of revolutions such as OWS, the Presidential campaigns, environmental movements, all these fail because no one ever sees the movement from the other person's point of view.

If this were true, the discussion in OWS meetings about how to bring the big banks and investment firms down would quickly be replaced by the greater good of directing all energy and strategies toward the goal of enacting future legislation that would ultimately be instated limiting certain conditions and powers. By the way, before you sit back and shout out "you're crazy". This kind of thinking is the backbone of the legislative process and well balanced laws. In all honesty, you should be asking yourself "What would the legislation include if it was written in laymen's terms?" I think this kind of approach while not very glamorous is real, productive and as a result is revolutionary. Furthermore, any notion that corporate America should be excluded from this table is absolutely preposterous! Think about it, people are suggesting that we revolutionize capitalism by ignoring it all together. Apart from instilling radical socialist or communist ideologies, people need to realize that this is a slippery slope and one the majority of Americans are not particularly accustomed to. While they may be accepted in Europe and to a lesser degree in Canada, the American way is diametrically opposite in every regard. Capitalism is not the problem, the problem is people thinking they can control everything people do. Let me ask you, do you believe in someone's ability to prove themselves and make more money than the rest of the people in the group? Do you believe that the government should charge everyone even if there is incredible abuse by many of the government systems that lead to deficits and debts? A large number of Americans will say no because they have grown up in a capitalistic society. And the idea that a revolution in the US could change that is just impossible. Now does that mean that I am saying that the OWS movement should come to a grinding holt? No, what it does mean is that you better clarify the business case (ie mission statement) and the sales pitch otherwise its GAME OVER. Especially when the economy starts picking up steam again, with housing prices returning to respectable levels, people will once again curl up with their old friend, capitalism.

Now if I was a member of the senior's population for example, an ever-growing demographic of American society, I may sympathize with those of the OWS movement but that doesn't mean they are going to go along with it. You must remember that these people were taught to believe in government as their protector and that the system however flawed it may be, is a "net-positive". Does your movement represent them? Are they implicated or included in any part by the movement? If they aren't you're overlooking a powerful lobby group. What about working men and women in their 30s and 40s or the baby boomers? Do they have a seat at the table? The idea here is to avoid drawing a line in the sand when it comes to division in a revolutionary cause.

The next question deals directly with your political standpoint. Why is it that everyone proudly wears their Republican or Democratic Emblin as though it were a Medal of Honor! It isn't, that's why the Medal of Honor is so respected! What your revolution must accomplish is exactly the opposite! If you want to create change invite your "enemy" at the discussions and battle it out! It may happen that his/her argument are better than yours and if it is the case, after serious consideration, you may actually have a consensus you can take to local, state and national governments irrespective of the camp the idea originated from. If you can't, then the political system will "imprison" any and all improvements to society. What I'm trying to say is, don't be played by political party loyalty. The goal is to change society for the better and if that means consorting with the enemy, who just may be the guy next door, do so in good faith that together you can make a change that will benefit all Americans as publicized through your sales pitch and stated in your Mission Statement. That's how you create change, that's how you elect new Presidents to replace the current ones, that's how you bring change to Wall Street! Remember, marches along Wall Street and Pennsylvania Avenue make for interesting reporting, but the submission of written proposals backed by a significant group of people ready to protest and raid the capital is the true recipe for successful revolution!

Tight casting from a revolutionary standpoint, is a slippery slope when you think about it, so if you do organize yourself this way, you better hold on tight because it's a long and treacherous way down!

Step 5

Dress rehearsal!

In this chapter you will learn:

- Your community is a dress rehearsal for the national/international stage – if you see that it doesn't work here, go back to the drawing board

- Remember – try to better your community through the movement but don't trash the place that shaped your thoughts and convictions – the idea is to make it better

- Along the way, stick to your guns on the principle issues, but take note of every constructive criticism you receive – those tend to teach you so much more than those simply tapping you on the back

- This will prepare you for the attacks on the grand scale when you go national or international with your revolution

- Treat every town/library meeting as s speech on the White House lawn – after all with today's technology it takes a second to be on CNN, Fox or BBC news

- One last thing – look the part but be a chameleon

Step 5

Dress rehearsal!

Everything in politics, sports, corporate America, is staged. It's all cleverly put together to create the illusion of grandeur, but innately we can detect when it's all smoke and mirrors because in each of these lackluster cases we are not "whisked" away by the campaign. In those cases we tend to be forced along in displaying our loyalty for the cause.

What people may not realize is that great politicians/leaders tend to make the link between importance, relevance and duty appear effortless. They somehow have fine-tuned the message to the point where it seems flawless and so natural that we could not help but be taken by its simplicity and impact. The only thing people forgot is that in order to reach that stage, there were thousands of dress rehearsals in town halls, pubs, gymnasiums and living rooms in which the candidate explained face to face why his or her ideas made sense. Why he/she could turn things around in their town or city.

You see long before President Reagan caught the attention of the world with a very captivating message, he rehearsed throughout his movie career. This allowed him to be calm in front of the camera but more importantly allowed him the opportunity to take the position as the President of the Screen Actors Guild where he addressed the issues of the day. Despite this experience, the greatest influence of all came during his days as a spokesman with General Electric (GE) where he travelled all over America talking about the product (and political issues of course) to everyday working people and giving the speech his own special touch. It was during those years that he rehearsed his role and fine-tuned the message he would later take to office as Governor of California and then into his 2 terms as President of the United Sates.

You may be thinking, that was President Reagan, but does it really make a difference in modern day revolutions like the OWS revolution, or the Environmental Movement? Well, it is obvious that such lessons would make a huge difference for the 2012 election campaign and all future election cycles but you must always keep in mind, as a leader or participant of a cause, that you and your revolution must pay your dues. It just so happens that one of the best ways to pay your dues is to make use of the perfect setting to fine tune your skills - your community.

Your community can and should be treated as the equivalent to the national stage. Your district and its race can take on the importance of a White

House run. After all, an election in your community is nothing less than a scaled down version of the presidential election! This misconception along with another fictitious and potentially fatal idea, that protests somehow magically materialize into law must be analyzed and dispelled from conventional thinking. Anyone capable of dissecting, breaking down and building up these 2 actions into tangible, understandable tasks has the greatest chance at producing lasting legal change in society. But then again each of these individual tasks must be repeated until the procedure is optimized!

Basically, this previous paragraph boils down to the fact that you must repeat, perfect and most importantly, take the role of the change agent in your community. In addition, let me be perfectly clear, throughout this process, you will make many mistakes and miscalculations but the beauty is, that they are relatively internal to your community. So make as many mistakes as you need to but once you get it together you can then take your message on the road throughout the district, state and country with the added knowledge that you understand what works and what doesn't and your are ready to roll with the punches.

The dress rehearsal will also convince you of your own position and that your time sacrificed regarding the fight was and is worthwhile. Throughout the life of the revolution you will be tested by a wide spectrum of questions, complaints, pot holes that surround your campaign by many respected individuals in your community. The emotion, long hours and concentration regarding the revolution will begin to become personal, real and create an assurance and feeling that you are truly making a difference.

There appears to be great truth in the idea that to be successful you must dress and act successful, so to be a revolutionary you must dress and act like a revolutionary, but don't get caught up with the idea of fighting the enemy in mountains and canyons, in the modern equivalent, an office up in the city skyline could be as treacherous as the mine fields of North Korea.

Furthermore, along the way, throughout your community and throughout the country, you will meet many people. One of your jobs will be to ensure that certain acquaintances, people who can really help your revolution come to life, be singled out, as it is in your best interest to court them and try to convince them of the validity of the movement. The prize is even sweeter when the individual is on the opposite side of the aisle, in which case you must somehow find a way to ally yourself with them through common ground to infiltrate the opponent's position.

That is why sometimes, being completely different from the establishment doesn't work. In general people in power tend to open up to those that are similar to them and if your opponent is a corporate executive, his or her patience with ragged looking people may be the nail in the coffin. On the other hand, a revolutionary dressed in sheep's clothing, arguing with the merit of a profit/loss argument, as well as with client displeasure leading to corporate losses, now there's an argument that gets to the heart or in this case pocket book of the big multinationals.

Before going any further, the dress rehearsals throughout you community are not what they once were. People can make mistakes at this grass roots level as I mentioned earlier but, due to modern technology, these can be propagated throughout the world over the internet. This was of course not the fact only a short time ago, so this can serve as both a blessing and a curse and as such is yet another fact of the dress rehearsal for the revolution. You see, you may not realize it but that last speech made with only 10 people in attendance, might be the one that gets viewed 10,000 times on YouTube and that becomes the characterization of the movement in your community. It is specifically cases such as these where your opponent will find those inaccuracies and use them against you. So dress like the enemy when meeting with them. Take on the persona of the senator/congressman ultimately signing the bill into law. Remember, a suit doesn't change the message it only makes it more pleasing and accepting to others in power and in the end, the congressmen and/or senators are the people who make the final decisions with their votes. So what more can I say than "Dress for success"!

Part of the collateral damage that takes place in any revolution be it the Environmental movement, the Presidential campaigns or OWS, the actual person at its head or those battling it out to represent the cause, will inevitably become the community punching bag. This is true on the small scale as well as on the national and international stage. That is yet another reason why it is so important to dress the part, simply because regardless of the outcome, your life will have been affected by your actions whether you realize it or not. What I want is for you to be both instrumental in leadership for the cause as well as take the experience with you as a building block for a life of protest or perhaps the start of your new life in the public eye. And if it so happens that you mutate into the establishment you once detested, this dress rehearsal will have provided you the sneak peak to prepare yourself to confront the temptations and inertia of political life and to recall the struggles of the "common man/woman" you once were!

Now the dress rehearsal is obviously based on the assumption that you already have a business case, mission statement, sales pitch and schedule for the revolution/election to take place especially since you will be disseminating this idea via your speeches and visits throughout the community, and state.

What you should be concurrently working on is your legal document. As I mentioned earlier in the step 4, the back bone of the document must remain separate from the actual legal document for quality assurance purposes to verify the checks and balances that exist between the mandate of your revolution and what actually appears on paper in the final analysis. This parallel operating scenario allows the electoral/legal side of the coin and the revolutionary side to move as 1 along the timeline. Such planning and action will account for the most timely and orderly conversion from the revolution (ie vision) to election and implementation into law (the new reality).

In the dress rehearsal step, your business case/mission statement, sales pitch and timeline must be a widely available file that all have access to and is of course the highlight of every speech from you the leader or any other participants of the revolution. On the other hand the actual legal document, both the backbone and the legal translation remain internal documents updated weekly and discussed amongst the upper brass. In the meantime, a monthly meeting should be held with the legal firm hired to continually make changes and update the text to accurately describe the terms and the possible conflicts that can occur with current legislation in force. In the case of the legal firm, hire a young, unemployed, hungry, lawyer starting out that wants to make his or her name with these kinds of case.

I truly believe that you are now beginning to realize what is taking place right before your very eyes? You as an individual have first proven to yourself the belief in an idea in your mind, heart and soul. You know that it is just and that the work must be done. You have come to terms with the idea that this change can take place but it will take a great deal of time, sacrifice and may cost you some friends while making more than a few enemies.

Then you and your peers, or comrades, whatever you call yourselves, created the business case the mission statement, sales pitch and schedule to achieve your goal. It is in this schedule that you realized that there were two sides to the coin. The revolutionary side – the vision that gives birth to a new idea and starts its growth followed by the election/ legal side (ie the new reality) that justifies its reason for being; this is where you probably started to get really excited since you then knew where and how to channel your energy magnifying it exponentially before our very eyes.

Then you begin to take on your role as the main character in this Shakespeare play, without the whole tragedy aspect of course. It is here where you become the salesman, the philosopher, the protector of the people. This is where you gain your confidence, where you fine tune your message, where you truly become one with the revolution (viva la Repubblica!)

Furthermore, you have already accepted the idea that your revolution, will NOT tight cast any characters that will bring it to fruition. You know that the wider the representation, spanning as many groups as possible, the easier it will be to force your elected officials into abiding by the will of the people, since your revolution will be representing the many facets of the population.

And finally, for the first half of the revolution anyways, you have from the very beginning rehearsed the part. You have acted out the drama in your own mind. You have played the role always looking forward through your words and actions and acted nobly with both the public and with the establishment that disagrees with your views. You have dispelled any idea of lack of leadership and to the contrary, shown that you are the leader and will work diligently and relentlessly to achieve the goals you believe will change the course of history for your community, company, state or country! It is through your work, persistence, actions and forward thinking that the people see the reality of the revolution. This is absolutely crucial as your effort will force the rest of the public to work as a unit to force their elected officials into action.

Now you are ready for the opposite side of the coin. So flip that quarter and make it happen – ***LEGALLY!***

Phase 2 Election:

(The "tales" side of the coin)

Step 6

Have the "movie script" (I mean the draft legal document) ready in advance

In this chapter you will learn:

- Don't forget - to change the world requires a written statement of what must be changed!
- The sales pitch is the target - but you will have to make concessions
- Young law school graduate(s) / Change / all under the marquee!
- All documents and revisions are Top Secret (for selected eyes only)
- Vision to major election platform – If not possible run for office yourself

Step 6

Have the "movie script" (i mean draft legal document) ready in advance

Recall that in step 5, I discussed creating 2 parallel documents, one with the essential (ie back bone) material required to achieve the Revolution's goals and the legal equivalent being created in parallel by a young hungry lawyer(s). Keep this in mind while I go off on a tangent for a second – Not surprised anymore are you?

If I asked you what was the greatest achievement of the American Revolution, (clearly one of the most important revolutions of history), you might scream out, the Boston Tea Party, the battle of Bunker Hill, or the infamous ride of Paul Revere. All of these of course influenced the revolution and made the dream that much more real in the minds of the American psyche but despite all of those incredible achievements, the actual creation of the Declaration of Independence and each of the Amendments that make up its content far surpasses all of those actions. After all most may not even be aware of these great battles and heroic actions but everyone knows the Declaration and its importance. Now before I continue, technically speaking, you could have a political change without a revolution, but if you have a revolution and there is no legal documentation to justify it, did it really happen? Not at all! I believe that history is overflowing with revolutions of groups and sects that disagreed with the status quo of the then current regime. It would be an overwhelming task just to accurately count all of the insurrections but on the other hand, the revolutions that gave birth to actual meaningful legislation that makes our life safer, more enjoyable, more profitable and overflowing with hope for the future, well those kinds of laws are few and far between. That is what the Declaration of Independence and equivalent documents around the world represent. They are the legal representations of those revolutions and because they exist we know that that particular revolution took place and was worthwhile. We know the American Revolution occurred, because even if an individual knows nothing of the sacrifice of the battles, they can stand in awe in the Rotunda of the National Archives Building and read the inspiring and empowering words written by those great men hundreds of years ago.

The purpose of this book is, that you the reader, being a protestor of political, corporate, or social

Have the "movie script" (I mean draft legal document) ready in advance

issues, including interoffice/work issues, realize that every revolution has 2 sides, just as a coin does and you must always have both sides in your vision during the planning process for any revolution or any change for that matter. Those who have failed were nearsighted and overtaken by one aspect but those who truly wanted to succeed had both on their minds and more importantly in their plans and schedules.

Step 6 helps awaken those delinquent of the legal aspects to catch up and realize that even if you happened to forget or completely ignored the legal side of it all, except if you read and are following the steps of this book of course, then you must get started and informed immediately!

In the end step 6 helps you come to terms with the fact that any revolution without change to the legal code, whether in a company workplace or the country at large, amounts to NOTHING – pure and simple! It is also true for politicians and corporate leaders who implement legislation without realizing that it should have been preceded or at least completed in parallel with a campaign/revolution for change to allow for a smooth transition and acceptance by a majority of their peers.

Think of it like this: the revolution would be the equivalent of the US election cycle, including the primaries and the entire general election, where as the legal aspect includes the voting day itself that legitimizes the candidate's power and all of the "promised" changes to society that can come about after the Republican or Democratic candidate take office. To bring it down to the nitty-gritty, imagine your boss at your workplace telling everyone that they had time to provide their input on changes that will come into effect in the next fiscal year and that you and your colleagues have then next two months to put together the list of changes/requests that are to be proposed to management regarding changes in the workplace.

Now if you and your group choose to be passive (ie forgo the revolution against those in power) then that means you would simply be force-fed the new rules, which is what most people do since it's the simplest response, and by the way, the one most appreciated by upper management. But what if a committee was created to represent the entire office, and they intern held discussions on a regular scheduled basis, and polled the workforce to accumulate accurate information? Then when the time comes, management better be ready for the assault because within the plans are the acceptance and willingness of work-to-rule, slow down and of course strike tactics! Do you see what I mean when I say all of life is a revolution? EVERY SINGLE TIME YOU STAND UP FOR AN IDEA, IT'S A REVOLUTION FOR YOUR VISION! Now in keeping with the example above, when the time comes and you come to the negotiation table well prepared with polling and employee requests along with the realistic list in your back pocket of course, you have now entered into the legal process that accompanies the revolution. This is where the "movie script" of the new law describing your beliefs becomes a reality and it is

Have the "movie script" (I mean draft legal document) ready in advance

only subsequent to this step that you can you look back at the work you have accomplished as a group!

I believe that just as oil floats to the top of a bucket of water, all of the important changes float to the top as the revolution is taking place. It is from this long list that you and your group get together and vote on the most important issues with a ranking system in place. This helps in the voting process as well as the discussions that take place within the group especially regarding the top 3 spots that are already ingrained in your sales pitch and Mission Statement. Even more importantly is the recognition that the opposing party, whether an employer, the local/state/federal government etc are all intent on giving you ABSOLUTLEY NOTHING, despite their actions or what they are saying publically. This should of course come as no surprise as companies belong to their shareholders, who usually have no relation to the actual workforce, while governments, when involved in the negotiation, will represent the so-called national interests which will inevitably be in stark contrast to yours!

Given the climate of distrust you must be ready in advance with the 1 to 3 central points of negotiation. The process is of course a tug-of-war that will go back and forth within your camp. It is your job to know which are the pawns and which pieces on the chess table are simply not in play. This is the biggest mistake most people make in any negotiation and that includes even the smallest negotiations like who does the dishes at home.

The idea is to include the extra points on your list as the buffer against the 1 – 3 issues that must be implemented. Now I say this because there are many unknowns among your opponents that are probably in direct conflict with your requests. Despite these, you must be ready to sacrifice or "appear to sacrifice" as much as possible in a display of your solidarity with the opponent even if it simply isn't the case. Furthermore, throughout the negotiation process, ensure that emotion is left at the door. It will virtually ALWAYS lead you to a dead end and so your leader, while passionate, must be one who can control and channel passion throughout the negotiation process – if he or she is unable to, have them rally the people outdoors as opposed to carrying out the conversation in the offices.

I spoke of this in earlier chapters but it must be repeated as this tends to be the Achilles heel of every change. You see the law is purposely written to be confusing. Every single word directs the reader in a different direction and must be verified. Now here is the ultimate disclaimer, "I am not a lawyer and every time I read a section of legal code I find myself reading it many times over and still have questions regarding the rule at the end of my effort" It is for this reason, you should consider asking a young lawyer fresh out of law school that is looking for experience, to help be an integral part of the revolution.

Now, I know being a lawyer tends to automatically flip a switch of florescent dollar signs but in reality many of them are out of work and are looking for projects to take on. Yours could be one of THE

Have the "movie script" (I mean draft legal document) ready in advance

projects that puts them on the map in your community and that displays to everyone the kind of character they have within and whether this is true or just a ploy is not important to you. What is important is the fact that you now have a legally trained expert as part of your master-mind group. Now if you are having a hard time recruiting that way, perhaps, you can provide a retainer fee from the group's budget that goes directly to the lawyer regardless of the work done. In this case, it may even motivate the group to work hard to ensure that the lawyer is earning their keep.

Another, possibility is to go to the local university and give a speech in an effort to recruit using the "Sales Pitch" for the goals that can be accomplished together with a lawyer's "esteemed intelligence and knowledge of the law", if they would be willing to take on the fight together. You could explain how they would be practicing what the law truly was meant for. To defend the rights of those who most need their help. They would in this situation, undoubtedly be the "saviors" of the revolution from the election/legal standpoint. I believe that student lawyers are just like other students activists plain and simple - before they take on their craft of course. So if you use your sales pitch to appeal to those who believe in changing society just like you, you'll have one or more or your greatest "soldiers" - after all who better to argue the law than those who understand and are most intimate with it. In the end if you truly want your revolution to make a difference if you truly want your vision to become reality you must find a way to channel their energy for the sake of the revolution you care for so deeply!

Another factor that impacts the revolution is the level of information housekeeping regarding the progress of the vision/revolution and its equivalent election counterpart. What is important to remember is the fact that everything must be recorded and controlled. This appears to be a rather foolish and obvious statement but in actuality, especially at the beginning of the movement's progress, it's important that ideas/strategies/notes and not-so-important notes (at least for the moment anyways) be recorded as these provide a log of the thought process progression and also eliminate the time and effort to recapture where the group stood as of the last meeting or get together. This also serves as a way to get new recruits up to speed on all the changes, or stagnation that have taken place. You see, one of the biggest problems of any movement is the ability for the leader to communicate the progress, share the tasks and empower others. One of the ways this occurs is through the leader's abuse of power through their control of the information coming in through meetings and side discussions. Now don't get me wrong, as the leader you must withhold some delicate information but at the same time information must flow swiftly towards those best equipped to magnify its importance, appeal and dissemination.

What people must recall, is that in the election/"new reality" phase, the ideas of the revolution that started the fire and initials flames, must be allowed to propagate quickly and savagely via word

Have the "movie script" (I mean draft legal document) ready in advance

of mouth, over the internet, through internal campaigns etc, etc. It happens quite often at this point that the leaders feels like he or she is losing their grasp and control over the situation and because of this feeling of loss of ownership, actually starts to become an enemy of the movement. This is precisely the reason for getting into the habit of taking minutes for all meetings and conversation from the very start of any revolution so that leadership is more group-based than individual based.

The second reason to have working, fluid document (ie: revisions) both public and secretive is so that periodically, every month or every quarter at most, the actual message and the eventual law that the movement (ie the group) is working on implementing gets refined to the point where it becomes doctrine. If I were to ask you, what separates a serious movement from an armature one? What would you say? Some might say it is emotion or belief in the cause. Others the feeling of belonging to the group while others might say that the group must be directly affected by the ongoing changes forced upon them by their company or country. These are of course all true and absolutely necessary but I think the most important is the demonstration to the entire group of the actual achievements and progress completed thus far and that such progress is directly accredited to the group's efforts and resilience to date! Let me ask you, when people with a weight loss objective go to meetings where they have all the information needed, along with support from others and the equipment to train and exercise why is it that nearly

99% will simply continue on their path to weight gain or simply not be able to decrease from their current weight? You see, as I just mentioned, all those extras are simply cherries on the Sunday, pardon the pun, but in the end what makes them truly believe they can lose weight is seeing their own progress, however small, before their very eyes. So in this example, as in any other, after they have been pushed forward by their "fire/vision" for physical change and start an exercise program, thereby overcoming the inertia of their obesity, they should then start to record their training and eating habits so that they begin to see actual weight loss over the past week, month and year. At that point seeing is believing – and the "New Reality" becomes simply a matter of time! You see, weight loss, just like election campaigns are very dependent on results or the lack there of which is the reason for their downfall. People expect accept for a select few, that they will be unable to pass through the threshold of the unknown and disbelief regarding their respective Goliath! So in the end, the best medicine for a doubting Thomas is nothing more than to place their fingers in the wound. In other words to see the progress that has taken place since the revolution took shape and at every stage along the way. Furthermore, such progress in the form of meeting notes, facts, information and voter feedback will also support the legal exercise by providing better evidence that will help create an ever improving draft of the New Law/Reality to come. Just one note, in the case of political and economic change, separate the common knowledge from the

Have the "movie script" (I mean draft legal document) ready in advance

sensitive/secretive facts and strategies all the while keeping 2 logs – the general log and its Top Secret counterpart. (Note: You may want to keep the negative facts a secret within the top brass until you find a use for it or a clever spin on the situation).

Another high level case where this process is followed religiously includes the election of a political candidate such as the republican candidate in the US Primaries or the support for the current President for his second mandate. In these cases, the election campaign progress in different districts, countries or states, can be easily reviewed through gallop poles, phone calls and the door-to-door campaign. Here general information is disseminated to all quickly but the actual anticipated legal agendas are kept secretive to a small internal circle. This same principle is equally applicable in more common situations such as company workers trying to instate a union to defend their rights on the job by formally voicing their grievances through recorded incidences in the manufacturing plant. It is true for the office worker who requests a raise in salary or the advancement of position and responsibility as well as a student who requests that they be given the opportunity to complete their project/thesis on a subject that they have been studying on their own time that can serve as a fascinating subject matter and relevant information for society!

I know this might seem strange, but if I was to ask you to create a flier or a brochure for the revolution/election (ie: vision/new reality) would you be able to summarize all you are working on into 1 sheet? Or perhaps a single emblem or flag?

This happens to be one of the most difficult of all exercise throughout the campaign. You see in order to get your idea into the form of a bill and then brought before congress and the senate, it must be of great importance to the people at large. Everyone reading this book must remember that unlike the multi nationals that have millions to invest in lobbyists to have their bills pushed through congress, we have neither the time nor the financial power to undertake this political exercise. As regular everyday citizens we must push with all our might to get the bill before the municipality to create change at the local level and then continue the momentum toward the state legislature and finally before congress and the senate. In spite of all the theoretical ways to bring about change, our best chance may be to frighten our elected officials into action by convincing people to show them the door to unemployment if they choose to ignore the cries of the people.

In the event that you realize after a campaign or 2 that despite your group's publicity and hard work that the opposing candidate has made it through regardless, you may choose to leverage the notoriety and publicity you built toward a run at public office. After all, your work may have proved to your friends and critics alike of your legitimacy and may have set you into a perfect position to propel your campaign forward as one of the candidate in the next election campaign.

If you did choose to run for office, you must realize that you will have to research the issues currently being addressed, including budget issues that will affect any future decisions. This of course adds a lot of work and will take a great deal of your time but you will present the position on a grand scale. Plus, all of your fellow revolutionaries would know that they may be part of something that will truly effect society and of course their own careers.

But before you lead the protest or think of running in an election, let's get back to this brochure idea once again, both hard and soft copy versions of course!

If you are not sure how to create a "brochure", speak with a friend, or a friend of a friend that majored in marketing and another that's a graphic artist. Explain to the marketing major what you're looking for and what might work best in your case. Work on it together and have fun with it; remember you're doing all this work because you want to see change. Then once you have this idea set up for the brochure and the website, then convey this to the graphic artist. You could of course do this as a single session which would be best but with this kind of work and people's busy schedules you never know. That's reality and we know there's no way around it! Furthermore, in this day and age, software packages are widely available making this quite simple so find the group member who is most familiar to lead the project with you and most importantly before you make the final decision have a vote on the best choices for both the brochure and website with all in the group in attendance. You want them to feel like they are part of a revolution and so during those moments where they get to sit in and help decide, these occasions will provide them the fuel they need to keep going in their respective tasks for the revolution!

Now apart from all the websites and brochures, there appears to be something subconscious about waving a flag. You can sense it at any sporting event, the Olympics, parades, ceremonies everywhere. They, regardless of the digital age we live in, seem to defy the laws and maintain their appeal. If you think about it, a flag that represents your cause is one of those underestimated but instantaneously understandable stamps of recognition and approval and more incredibly once waved around by supporters of any cause, become somehow the a vocal powerhouse even when society does not give you the chance to explain your cause. All protestors have to do is unite in protest, chant their beliefs and wave the flag of change. In the 1960's the flags waving with peace signs told those far and near who was protesting why and what it was about before any discussions ever took place. More importantly, it has ingrained in it, a military feeling. A feeling of strength that comes from a people unified in their belief. Even the maniacs of history knew that it made for great marketing and solidarity and yet people and revolutions tend to overlook one of the simplest tools of marketing ever created. You might want to get one of your guys working on this right away.

Now let's get back to the 2 major documents, one being the document for change in laymen's terms and the other its legal clone that will be raped and pillaged throughout the legislation process. Because

Have the "movie script" (I mean draft legal document) ready in advance

of the distortion between the two major documents the mission statement must be written in everyday words, must be concise, simple but not overly simplistic and above all EXACT in what victory is and should represent.

I believe it happens all too often that when the law works its magic or black magic depending on how you see it, the original intent often gets lost in translation. The list of questions I included below will help shape your vision of victory and make the message concrete so that all can understand what your group is after. At the end of it all, you can use this same list to test the final legal document against your vision in the ultimate litmus test for truth.

Legal statutes versus our vision for change:

1. What is the problem? What are you rebelling against?
2. What is the purpose of the revolution? What do you want to achieve?
3. Why is this law needed in the first place?
4. What is expected by the government and the people if the law is enacted?
5. When should this law come into effect and will it have retroactive enforcement?
6. Who is affected by its incorporation into the legal code of the town/city/state/nation?
7. What penalty will an entity (individual or corporation) will have to pay if considered in violation?
8. Where will this law will be enforced (community, statewide, national)?

9. Have any federal laws or amendments in the US constitution been broken by either party involved?

Example: Secure funding to design and build a modern library facility in your town

1. The current library is completely useless! There should be a new modern facility that will allow everyone in town access to information and learning products to advance their possibilities of employment as well as enjoy the activity of reading, (not a relic that has become useless to society and wastes taxpayer money for nothing).
2. The purpose is to urge the local government to set funds aside to build a new facility or overhaul the current building to ensure that it becomes the modern facility that will help society as well as a place that all people will enjoy and make use of.
3. In this case, a motion would have to be accepted by city council to ensure that a study be completed to define the cost of both possibilities and that the motion then be passed to begin the construction of the new building or the renovation of the current one with an exact timeline and chosen contractors for the work.
4. The city will expect that its citizens pay the additional cost in their taxes over the next 5 or 10 years depending on the cost of

construction. The people in tern expect a functioning building within a 2 year time span.
5. The tax increase will take place immediately after the decision to begin construction and end in the allocated timeframe.
6. All of the community will be affected by the construction or renovation of the new library via tax increases.
7. No new penalties except for everyone's acceptance of the tax increase.
8. The increase tax hike will be within the municipality alone (or possibly part of the statewide budget), whichever is more efficient from a tax purpose (to be decided by city accounting board).
9. No amendments of federal state/district-county law have been jeopardized by the final acceptance or rejection of the people's request for a new library.

I used a library example because I wanted to show that the thinking process is the same for a library as it would be for the threat of war in a foreign country. At the heart of any action, every person must ask themselves these questions in order to clarify what it is they really want to achieve and what that will entail from both sides. Furthermore, the questionnaire's simplicity and directness will ensure that you do not lose sight despite all the fog and haze surrounding these issues. Most importantly, when all of the emotion and anger from the big issues facing us start setting in, this kind of checklist will help set you straight and judge for yourself whether you and your revolution are on track or not.

Lastly it serves as a "check and balance" against the legal document that exits the grinding machine at the other end of your revolution/election process. If that document does not correlate with this test, that is the point when you will be forced to decide if it is "truthful enough" for you and your group/organization to accept and proclaim as victory. I say his because I wrote this book for real life not fairy tales and at a certain point you will have to make this decision yourself; so be ready for an iterative process that may drive you and your crew absolutely insane!

In the end, revolutions/visions and elections/New Realities are all about the "script"!

Step 7

Negotiation, negotiation and more negotiation!

In this chapter you will learn:

- If you are not a good negotiator, you may win the battle but you will ultimately lose the war

- Hone your skills in this department – or you are guaranteeing a loss

- 11 Negotiation Tactics

- Timetable

- Great negotiators size their enemies, have you?

Step 7

Negotiation, negotiation and more negotiation!

Quickly, if I was to ask you to role play in a discussion in which you take the place of your boss, the other political party, the big bank executives or whoever represents the opposition in your case, what do you think you (as the "big cheese") would be ready to forfeit in an actual negotiation?

Answer = NOTHING!

You see now that you are in their shoes, you realize that every little thing you give up amounts to a loss to the shareholders or the treasury or your bottom line as boss/executive. In the end it's all about the balance of power in the relationship and if you were to be brutally honest you would do and act exactly as they would if you were in their shoes. I say this because negotiations have nothing to do with emotion and everything to do with human nature. It's why humanity is always in a struggle with itself and why very few are ever really happy.

Think about it, in cases where there is mutual agreement between 2 parties, which for all intensive purposes is the best of scenarios because the agreement may actually hold for the term noted in the contract, even in this case, the truth is, both parties did not get what they actually wanted. This sounds quite negative when you think about it and is only so, because most people involved in any negotiation from the least influential all the way to a UN vote for sanctions and military incursions, tend to all ask for too much and forget that there is in actuality really only 1 or maybe 2 objectives to achieve throughout the entire discussion. Sometimes the true objective is simply to maintain the status quo!

You see the great negotiators, of which you should be extremely interested, are able to turn and twist a discussion in such a manner that they achieve those 1 or 2 objectives while giving up pseudo objectives of minor importance. In other words, short of actual weapons, negotiations are wars plain and simple. People of course come in dressed well and wearing a smile but the stakes are high and the battle front has been prepared. What you and your revolution have to remember is that as the underdog you just as your opponent must be extremely well prepared to take on the attacks from the other side.

If I had a quarter for every employee who rushes in to their boss's office with a prepared speech in their minds explaining to him or her why they deserve an immediate raise without an actual report, timeline, sales figure or presentation to justify such action, I'd be a millionaire! In the same token, in every OWS rally I have seen or read about, never have the protestors proposed or requested a single change that can actually be instated. On the political front, it is quite the opposite but amounts to the same end. Politicians running for President, Congress or Senate all promise that they will change the world, decrease the debt by unimaginable and incomprehensible amounts and all within the first 100 days of office! In all of these cases the common thread that links all these problems is that they lack a singular vision and proof for their reasoning and as a result they are unable to negotiate because they are unwilling to give anything up. And since both sides are coming in with the same mind set nothing ever gets done.

In negations on the grand scale such as government debt reductions via the increase of tax payments, major union strikes, polling provides the most accurate information possible. You have to remember, these scenarios deal with thousands and sometime millions of people and as such they must be polled in a manner that makes sense. Now I tend to agree with the information assembled but so many times it appears to not make any sense at all. This is where your common sense must act as the final filter of the data retrieved. At the same time though, it is also very possible that you as leader or your council as a whole, may not agree in the validity of the data retrieved, and it may happen that you are in fact wrong! It does happen I assure you! Regardless of the scenario, you as the head of the revolution along with your council must come to a decision after retrieval of this information as to what your number 1 objective is and this must be unanimous as it will be your guiding light in any negotiation process.

In actual negotiation, there are a few key pointers to keep in mind but before I continue, this is only the beginning of a study that will help you throughout your lives in everything from work, to shared tasks with your spouse. I therefore urge you to conduct your own study of negotiation tactics but I do want to provide a list of ideas to begin with.

1. Always know the 3 things you want! (it might be more but you must be realistic of course).
2. Of the 3 - know their order of importance - in particular the MOST IMPORTANT OF ALL.
3. Have at least 10 scenarios of what can happen laid out on the table for which you have the response prepared in advance (the more powerful your opponent, the more scenarios you should have covered).
4. Of the 10 scenarios half should be of negative consequences with the 3 WORST cases known by all your group.
5. Know whether you have the support of your group to make the final decision if a particular scenario is reached or whether you have to return to the huddle to discuss the decision.
6. Many times, when negotiations drag on, it can become very costly to the employer – time and patience may be a valuable weapon for you. Use this as much as you can!

Negotiation, negotiation and more negotiation!

7. Start off with the intent of increasing the momentum of agreement and good will by:
   a. Agreeing on milestones together that break the final decision into phases
   b. How to keep record of the decisions made to date
   c. How to explain the progress to the public throughout the negotiation process
      i. These lead to TRUST which is essential in negotiation
      ii. And help remove the FEAR that makes people become more and more rigid in their stance
8. Remember, no one can quantify exactly what will occur through the different scenarios and so you will have to go by feeling at a certain point (but never let your opponent know this)
9. If you are not sure or sense a sudden decline in the atmosphere - call a recess based on a completely different reason or adjourn the meeting till tomorrow
10. If you have cornered your opponent based on your arguments or purely out of chance, employ one of your predetermined scenarios immediately; (hopefully one of your top 3, but that is for you to judge)
11. Lastly, always keep in mind that people usually fight and bargain even harder when they are unable to quantify the changes that will come about through the adoption of changes to the current rules. (this is true for both sides)

I believe that this list is one that is part conceptual and part common sense but it has worked for me on many occasions and in all sorts of scenarios. Always ensure that you have these 11 tactics of negotiation covered!

In ours or any case as you might expect, the two documents (laymen and legal) are the reference documents for the negotiation exercise with your boss/employer, the opposing political party, or the big banks in the case of the OWS movement.

The next exercise formulates the process for you and your group by providing a common example that all employees can use:

Tactics 1 and 2: Objective:
a) Promotion to Manager with the applicable salary increase
b) Salary increase by 5 to 7%
c) Salary increase between 3 to 5%

Tactics 3 and 4: 10 scenarios of what can happen	
i) Promotion to Manager with the applicable salary increase	i) Happy
ii) Salary increase by 5 to 7%	ii) Happy
iii) Salary increase between 3 to 5%	iii) Happy
iv) Salary increase between 1 to 3%	iv) Happy

Negotiation, negotiation and more negotiation!

v) Salary increase in line with inflation approx 2%	v) Acceptable
vi) Negligible increase (0.5 – 1%)	vi) Angry but you will accept
vii) Pay freeze for the year	vii) Angry – take action in accordance with the plan
viii) Decrease salary by 1 -2 %	viii to xv) Not acceptable - take action in accordance with the plan
ix) Big decrease in salary of 2- 5% x) Reduction in healthcare and dental benefits xi) substantial increase in the health and dental care premiums xii) Possible major layoffs to come and you will have to work more xiii) Your position may be terminated in the next 3 to 6 months xiv) Your position is terminated as it is decided that keeping your job here is no longer profitable xv) Subsequent to a review with the union, you will be let go immediately (by the way I actually came up with 14 scenarios here)	

Tactic 5: Gather group support
Speak with your spouse to know when enough is enough and when it may be time for you and your group to go on strike
You will have to be prepared financially for a prolonged stalemate
Make sure she/he knows all the outcomes including the worst of the 3.

Tactics 6: Time as a weapon
In this case, your boss may have the upper hand as he has all the time in the world.
You may be able to turn this in the form of "work to rule" or simply working slower or less effectively on purpose so that he understands that there are consequences for the purgatory you find yourself in.

Tactic 7: Ways to increase the momentum
Agree on milestone to judge your work performance
Keep a record of the notes/decisions made
Explain the progress of your projects at the upcoming meetings with your boss.
Discuss with colleagues regarding their salary increases with their bosses to compare scenarios if possible

Tactic 8:
Keep your own notes as well as information related to body language regarding your requests for your own personal file.

Tactic 9:
If you see that the meetings are becoming confrontations take a breather and say you have to get back to his project that at this moment "takes precedence over everything including our meetings regarding my salary increase"
OR the alternative
Continue on in the hope that he/she will crack under pressure. This is a case by case decision – with experience you will come to understand these breaking points more quickly and how to react

Tactic 10: If you are successful in Step8 and 9 then
Ask that he/she formalize the request to Human Resources/Payroll for the increase and to cc you in the email by the end of the week (ie there must be an actual date of completion to confirm)

Tactic 11:
Noted throughout the process

This same scenario can be rehearsed for the 2012 Republican primaries, for the 2016 Primaries for both Democrats and Republicans should President Obama win a second term. For the OWS movement, city by city, to know what they are in fact fighting to achieve, what they are willing to accept and what they believe should occur to make their risk-to-reward worthwhile.

Now I'm not saying that this is the end of the road! That once you have this table go ahead and call it a day. What I am saying is that this table puts your goal into perspective and allows you as the leader of a revolution or group to shape your ideas and actions into negotiation tactics and a document that summarizes the progress. This table will of course refer to Word, Excel and PowerPoint files explaining in greater detail what the specific actions are for each sub-step, but it will most certainly help you at the start of your fight when the movement must overcome its fiercest enemy - inertia.

The next exercise is to create this same table for your goal. And by the way this same thinking can be used as a timeline for your career aspirations and even career changes. So go to www.silvioguadagnino.com and get a copy of the template to start creating your own negotiation tactics.

Now, draw a horizontal line and subdivide it in two. Then subdivide these 2 lines into 12 parts each. Within the 12 subparts, include the actions you will take in each of the months to create the change your revolution is fighting for. You will quickly realize whether you are being too aggressive or whether you're being too lazy or anywhere in between along the spectrum. You could even think of it as a puzzle in which you have to fit in the pieces onto a timeline; a timeline you MUST uphold not for anyone else like your boss but to achieve the goal you and your revolution believe in. Last time people got together like that, the first Black President was inaugurated, so it's obvious anything can happen if you believe in it and more importantly prepare and schedule properly for it such that it is achievable and in line with the recourses available.

The other point I want to make is crucial. Part of winning in negotiation processes is realizing that firstly you have to work your hands to the bone simply to get a seat at the table with the decision makers but then once at the table, you then have to realize and prepare yourself for the idea that they want absolutely nothing to do with you and your cause; they do not want to help in any way and certainly they do not want to aid financially or take on financial losses in any way, shape or form. I think that many people believe that once you are in a meeting with these decision makers that they will for some reason realize the importance of their decisions because of the rowdy crowd outside that's screaming for peace or environmental change that will affect the future of the country! This is a trap that is ingrained in all who watch too many movies. This illusion will cost you dearly in time, energy and money spent on the movement as well as your freedom if illegal action is taken at any time during the process.

This awakening to the reality of the situation will allow you to create sound arguments with that type of opponent in mind. Your arguments will have to be bullet proof backed by both fact and logic in addition to the cutting edge marketing required to get the general public on your side. It is for this reason that I would hope that anyone involved in the OWS movement for example, weigh the Risk/Reward ratio before being brought into a police station and booked with a crime without ever even knowing what the movement wanted to achieve. What I am advocating against, is the idea of the blind leading the blind!

Perhaps the most interesting negotiation process takes place in politics and of course during Presidential Elections. The strange part is that this negotiation process is unquestionably the most puzzling. This is one of those cases where negotiations with the over 330 million strong US population takes place every single day, with the passage of every law, or the continuation or cancelation of military incursions, and the passage of new tax legislation. You see this is a tangled web since you may agree with one candidate on tax code reform and then with another on their foreign policy and yet despite your belief in both you are forced into making a decision on a 1-candidate-fits-all scenario. Now in cases such as these when the 2 parties do not provide any tolerance for their party faithful, what you end up getting is a party within a party. And do not make the mistake of thinking that these sub-parties can be controlled. The last time a party made that mistake led to the creation of the Tea Party. That same thinking caused Ross Perot to run for office in 1992 and nearly create an upset. What happened in these cases is quite simple to describe; it was a REVOLUTION! Politicians prefer to use other words to describe the movement but the Tea Party was and is a revolution. What needs to be learned here is that if people have something to say, and they decide to frame and voice the message properly to the people over a sustained period of time (ie the negation process with the public) they can bring about sweeping change (ie: revolution) via our election process that still allows for this; although I must admit, it is nowhere as simple as it once was!

What I am trying to say is that the greatest of politicians are in reality the greatest negotiators. Even the absolute madmen of history like Hitler and Stalin, despite their atrocities, at a certain point in time these same individuals managed to convince a small group of people of their beliefs and intent and were hell bent on their plans. Then that fire spread until they became the figures of history we know them to be. So as a student of negotiation, whether you enjoy politics or not, you can learn a great deal about the art of negotiation by the way this select group of people argue.

Now as a political supporter, begin by negotiating with yourself. Do this by creating your own table as I did earlier and PROVE TO YOURSELF that you truly do believe in the stance you have and are currently taking! You might surprise yourself. Remember that President Regan may be known as a Republican President but he was a Democrat before that, until he made the change. Now in your case, it may be the opposite but that is not important. What is important is that you understand why you believe what you do and be able to vocalize your beliefs so that you can convince others around you of your ideas and by extension campaign and provide support for your candidate. Best part is, if you do complete this exercise, imagine how much more credible you will be on the campaign trail and who knows, you may be practicing for a future campaign when you do decide to throw your hat into the race.

In the end your ability to negotiate will lead to the most powerful force in the political arena – numbers. And numbers mean everything in this business and in any revolution for that matter! They even count more than the message does in most cases, (sadly), as is seen nearly every election cycle!

Now, I want you to complete one more exercise amongst your group before you go to your next protest or debate. Ask one of the group members, perhaps one that appears to continually test your leadership, to have a debate where they represent the enemy and can fire back just as the enemy would. In addition to the actual battle of the minds, the energy between the two of you will help size your opponent and may be equivalent and perhaps even more toxic than your relationship with the enemy, better preparing you in your debate (ie negotiation) with the your opponent.

Ultimately, these exercises are all ways to allow you to fine tune the most important part of the "tales" side of the coin for your group's revolution for change. Any true leader must ensure that he or she is well versed in this type of modern, social warfare and I hope this chapter at the very least got you thinking about your abilities on this field of battle.

Step 8

Leverage hard fought battles - it's all in a day's work!

In this chapter you will learn:

- People love to hear about the journey to the top of the mountain and they enjoy it even more when it will affect them positively

- They will trust you because you represent them completely

- Ally yourself with congress, but always ensure that the change is yours

- If you can keep the revolution grounded in real every-day change then the fire will burn for ages

- As expected – you must publicize over the internet via blogs, Facebook, Twitter etc but don't ever forget the human touch

Step 8

Leverage hard fought battles - it's all in a day's Work!

Have you ever heard a revolutionary speak about the journey that led to the final victory that the people enjoy every day and usually take for granted? Do you see the way their eyes light up? The way their hearts, minds and souls are somehow transported to another time and space and then after a brief pause that in their eyes probably represents a lifetime, they begin to recount from the very beginning how the scattered pieces of the puzzle came together to create what is undoubtedly the defining moments of their lives.

Ask or read about anyone who fought on D-Day, or protested during the civil rights movement. Anyone who was involved in the overthrowing of government in the Arab springs, the creation of the new constitution for the Italian Republic subsequent to WWII.

This is as true for the forefathers of the American Revolution and the Declaration of Independence as was true for Castro's Cuban revolutionary movement to overthrow Batista's government. It is the same for the Environmental movement which has made great progress over the last 20 years and was undoubtedly the case when American voters elected their first black President. We live in incredible times, there is no question, but while your revolution is in the trenches, figuratively speaking, you need to be able to market to new recruits, to command media attention via the web, radio, TV, articles, blogs, YouTube, basically any and every way to convince the people that your movement has legs. That your movement is making progress; progress that far surpassed your schedule and not to mention your hopes and dreams.

You see everyone wants to have been part of a great revolution, an efficient 10-step revolution being best of all; a revolution that led to the discussion table that finally legitimized the requests into actual law, applicable to all citizens. At this point, I believe that with all the progress you made in the previous steps, you should now check the so-called "realism" at the door, respectfully of course. You see, the best way to understand this is simple, in any revolution even scheduled ones such as Presidential election coming up, requires a positive outlook. If you look back at the 2008 Election when Barack Obama won the race for the White House, I believe that he tried to paint a picture to everyone of what he would actually do in his speeches but in all honesty the everyday voter tends to overlook, distrust and most often despise any promises made by politicians especially in an election year, but in President Obama's case the chants of "Yes we can", "it's time for change, positive change", rang loud throughout the American landscape to the point that it didn't matter how he was even going to get this done! The people stopped asking for the process because they had been fed the story line with a thickening plot of better days to come. What you have to understand is that for any change, the revolutions and elections that legitimize the fight, are anything but realistic and if you are to get your revolution completed, be it the OWS movement, a new job, overcoming an addiction, getting your candidate voted into office you have to bypass the realism at a certain point, temporarily of course. If you are really not comfortable with this strategy then all you have to do is look behind you at all your progress and perhaps add more time to your schedule with a better description of the individual tasks that will eventually lead to your final goal. This should help convince you to convince your audience that the great message for change while grandiose is coming, whether they believe it or not.

Even more important, the reason this idea is so important is because people love stories about the resistance your group faced along the way! They love to hear about the hardships and sacrifice and you know why? We live in a movie/Hollywood based society where the plot must be enticing and filled with peaks and troughs. Future supporters need to know that you and your revolution were on your knees; that you summoned your last ounce of energy and dime that created the momentum to finally pass the finish line. Then if some or many happened to be hurt or die during the movement the Hollywood plot simply thickens with suspense and intrigue. Crazy I know; but in life, just as in film you have to leverage these battles through your message and medium.

If you think about it, have you ever heard a story or scenario told by a person simply giving you the straight facts and that same story told by a magical storyteller? As a kid we knew who could recount to us the greatest stories; we would jump on them the moment they said "okay are you ready for the story about the night in the dark forest that made his way to treacherous castle to save the princess". Absolutely, so do you really think that anything changed between then and now?

Basically the start of this chapter, the 8th step of the 10-Step Revolution amounts to a single piece of advice – the ability to explain your sales pitch as an exciting and moving short story describing the revolution to date leading to its climactic ending – to the point where it could almost be turned into a Hollywood blockbuster! There is nothing worse than getting to the election side of the coin (ie the "New Reality" side of the process) and all of a sudden being unable to explain what you had to go through to get to that point or being unable to arouse the people with what has been accomplished so far. You would be losing those perfect opportunities to capitalize and garner further support for your cause.

Leverage hard fought battles - It's all in a day's Work!

The beauty of being the leader/spokesperson of the revolution is that you, just like them are a person. I say this because in the last 30 to 40 years there are very few movements headed by actual people anymore! Think about it, in the past when we spoke of great ideas that changed our lives there tended to be a man's face attached to it. Whether it was Thomas Edison's light bulb, or the Wright Brothers first flight or JFK's demand for an American man to walk on the moon by the end of the decade, what was important was that it was a person. In the modern day everything is headed or championed by corporations and so movements tend to lose their human appeal. Whether it is an aircraft, or a new medicine it is always a company and this takes away some of the shine form the movement/invention. This is of course understandable as the amount of financing to create some of these great changes is monumental. On the other hand, if you step back and think about it, Microsoft being one of the most influential corporations on earth is different because Bill Gates was the revolutionary behind the phenomenon and it really was this man and more importantly that face that people see when they run any of his software around the world. The same is true for Apple; Steve Jobs is one of the most recognizable faces when he was alive and even more so now that he's passed on and that list goes on to include other game changers like Barack Obama and even such journalists like Julian Assange the creator of Wikileaks.

What I am trying to say, is that you as the leader or as a member of the movement must give it the personal touch to leverage the energy of the people and make them realize that they, just like you, belong to the revolution; That the revolution just like its "face" passed through trials and tribulations to achieve its goals. That this revolution cannot go forward without these people joining the fight. What this amounts to is TRUST plain and simple. As you might expect the majority of Americans and citizens of any country around the world for that matter have become very cynical of the behemoth banking, investment and government institutions that were responsible for the current recession that we have felt over the last 5 years. At least in government's point of view, there is a face, the President, and the people can revolt through the election process to bring about change but in the case of corporate America that is not so easy.

Very often people believe that when you are fighting for change that the government and your local officials are against you; that they always represent a form of resistance. Now this is true because the actions of any government representative will be scrutinized to no end by the public when they actually do decide to make changes and so they act slowly and cautiously which in many cases is both logical and sensible. On the other hand to make enemies with this or any powerful group is always discouraged. In the case of the local government, try to be civil at all times to ensure that the deviation in opinion doesn't become a personal battle against one another.

This might seem contradictory as movies are filled with scenes where the leader of a group rushes into the government legislature and screams for change. But if you watch the "unedited" version it would have shown that the people tried in every known way to provide the incentive for governments to make changes. This frustration with change, at the government level anyways, is the reason for the internet's very popularity and relevance – we as a people simply hate to wait for anything! What you have to remember is that even though the rest of the world has accelerated to internet speed, government change has retained its historical pace, and in fact requires much more persistence and patience than ever before.

It is for this reason that the 8th step of the 10-Step Revolution should include the idea of allying yourself with government as much as you can. In fact, if you can, get into government by running for office or get to know those who will be taking key positions in the near future – Just do it! Be as familiar and as cozy with the "enemy" as you are with your own group, all the while being cautious of the enemies allure. And believe me the power, influence, respect and security that comes with being a member of government is quite intoxicating, so be very cautious of your relationship.

Furthermore, if the opponent sees you more as a person, understands you and your revolution's struggle and how it effects those government officials and their families personally then they will slowly, very slowly, start to see that your opinion while different from the status quo does make sense and may be applicable. These are the important battles that allow you to win the war! I would have to argue that corporations are much more difficult to infiltrate with your message but the idea is still applicable.

In the case of corporations your idea, whether the change is economical, social, or anywhere along the spectrum, must be translated into a business plan for its message to gain traction. Plain and simple! Luckily you have a "draft" copy from the previous steps. In this scenario, you must take your revolution and convert it to financial figures that will affect their bottom line. This is your opportunity to make the great struggle one where the people will end up needing their company's services to make their life easier for example! In doing so you are beginning to speak to them in a language they understand and that they consider important. Now before I continue, come to terms with the notion that corporations do not need to care about people but they must and do care greatly about the people's needs! That should come as no surprise to anyone but so many forget this fact in their message, medium and leveraging tactics.

Keeping in mind the example of Corporate America, if we now consider the case of the OWS movement, they have no business case at all. If protestors think that people walking the streets will scare these guys, then the movement is wrong! You see stopping just one of the behemoth investment firms is harder than you think and even if you were successful, all its assets would simply be sold to its competitors adding to their balance sheets thereby giving them even greater power than they had before! Plus let's be honest these companies do have a place in society, especially for all those people who want others to manage their retirement funds and assets not to mention the huge number of people they directly and indirectly employ. In the case of big banks and institutions, their money comes from the savings and investments of people working in the community's they operate. So in the end, if you can ally yourself with your opponent through the proper message and medium (ie: by speaking their "language") you stand a much better chance of achieving a mutual goal as opposed to the most probable outcome – failure.

We all know that the internet is the way people get most of their information. Google itself is what everyone I know uses and is what I use to find almost anything and anyone. So technically anyone should be able to find and learn about your revolution and the updates on the legal front from your site. Now in the case of national or international movements such as Presidential campaigns, Green Peace for the Environmental movement or OWS movements, there obviously must be a way to update the marquee site with your information. But this is usually very difficult so you must create your own site that takes the international flavor and information and brings it home. This will make it "real" for the people in your community as opposed to the generic information about helping the polar bears in the arctic. Another example would be the translation that took place when OWS became Occupy Chicago, Occupy Rome, Occupy Toronto and Occupy San Diego. They took the idea and then tailored it to make sense for those involved in the local movement by adding their own spin on it.

Think about it, in the case of environmental movements, there is so much damage taking place everywhere that I would much rather hear about what can be done to help clean the river in my area for example than what is taking place in the arctic. That's not to say that I don't care about the arctic but the reality is that most people given the problems and concerns they have, will not even give it a second thought! I'm just being honest! But that same person would be absolutely infuriated if he or she knew that the local river from which water is purified had reached dangerous levels due to environmental pollution. Now if you could dig up this kind of so-called public knowledge and really make it public by bracing it on the "local edition" of the international website, that would really turn heads and minds. Of course always double and triple check any information before posting it on any site especially the "local" edition of an international site. (You could even think of your website as your very own New York Times)

Basically, what I am getting at is that you have to make sure that your movement, both the medium and the message touches them; that their every moment of inaction directly affects their health or the wallet or their individual rights. Once you are able to explain the situation in ways that matter to the people you see every day, at that point you will be able to build an army to march against the enemy and this will become crystal clear during the voting process when you and your organization apply the pressure needed to change the status quo.

It's also extremely important that you realize that only a decade ago there was a very limited form of communication available. If you championed an issue it was through telephone calls, letter campaigns, fliers and appearances. That meant that you were limited to the number of people you could gather in a given amount of time. But in the digital age not only can you attract the people in your municipality, state or county to your revolution, you could then easily acquire the support of neighboring areas and statewide/nationwide support as well. Perhaps one of the greatest destabilizes for both the revolution/vision and election/new-reality phases remains the ease with which a protest march can be started. It can be as simple as a text that went viral through the funneling of requests to all contacts, or a message that made its way through the millions of connection in Social Media via Facebook and Twitter.

There is a saying I keep repeating that "all politics is local" and at no time in history, was this saying more true. The difference now is that because of the internet age "local" has two meanings. It now includes the entire spectrum from your community to half way around the world, but in spite of this flexibility the messages can easily become lost, misunderstood or completely ignore due to all the noise. What you need to remember is that this power must be manipulated throughout your movement's election process with local government as well as during the revolution that preceded it. Your site, Facebook page, Twitter and blog sites must take advantage of the national information about the political party's show of force in the primaries for example and frame it into a debate that matters to the locals, all the while always making reference to your sales pitch for change and the legal document prepared that is in the process of being presented to local and state governments. If you do this, it almost seems like you are a chameleon - the local voice with the state-wide or national agenda in mind. This mix is what is needed at this point in the schedule as you and your group are gunning for change in the district, state and across the nation.

If you really think about it, the internet is really a medium that will allow you to leverage an idea and create a force that not even government or business can stop. BUT and this is the most important part to understand, you must have the proper foundation first. You must know what it is you are requesting EXACTLY, you must have a sales pitch/storyline that hooks the people and actually matters to them. You must then get them to mobilize as a group, and show up in great numbers to ensure that those in power are worried about the revolution and its affect on them and you must have the accompanying documentation to present at the proper time. I guess another way of describing it is that the internet is basically a machine that amplifies the input. The only problem is, if the input is garbage what do you think will come out!

As for the latest methods and wizardry in internet marketing, the web is full of how-to books with limitless strategies available; this chapter on the other hand, serves to explain the importance of connecting people with the struggle by leveraging both the message and medium. Only then will your movement become as real to others as it is to you!

Step 9

The "Schmooze" Factor

In this chapter you will learn:

- After you have built up momentum, contact listings, a platform – get some big names to come by and really get the ball rolling for the cause

- Big names sell tickets at the movies, politics/your revolution is no different

- Appeal to the party that aligns with your ideas – get to know the players – you might even want to run in the future – you never know!

- By the way, contrary to popular belief, the establishment is very attractive place to be!

- The mayor of your city, the local sports hero, one of the local businesses, the local veterans group

- Power by association – will inflate both your influence and your ego

- You have to tweak your pitch to suit them and their needs by answering the lifelong question "What's in it for them" – If you don't have this covered don't even try contacting them!

- The biggest mistake people make – courting those they already have!

Step 9

The "Schmooze" Factor

In all revolutions and their corresponding elections, perhaps your greatest weapon may be the "Schmooze Factor". That's right after building up all this momentum, creating 2 parallel flowing documents, the negotiation process, publicizing the road traversed to get to this place, what then gives you and your revolution/election the slight edge over other movements is the ability to attract the big names to increase the momentum of the movement to an unstoppable juggernaut.

What I'm saying here doesn't automatically mean that you will need to get Angelina Jolie to back your campaign, which of course if you can, would be very helpful from the general public standpoint. What I really mean is getting those key lawmakers such as the Governor, State senator, or the Attorney General, or a high ranking official at a government agency such as the Food and Drug Administration. Of course the best high profile people depend on the type of movement. In the case of the Presidential Election process, the ability to have the backing of other Governors and Senators is crucial to the support they need during the primaries and of course in the general election.

Now sadly, it turns out that even the most important issues tend to come down to what I like to refer to as the "schmooze factor" or "high School Election Phenomenon". I say this because in any type of movement possible, most will lose their momentum because at a certain point without the right faces bracing the front pages of campaign flyers, websites and TV ads, they will not be able to overcome the powers that be. I know it appears to be very pessimistic but look at any example in any movement. There is always one person that stepped in and made it mainstream. A perfect example is the environmental movement. This is by any standard the MOST important movement to all of humanity. It affects our very lives and the lives of the generations to come. Can anyone anywhere really disagree with what we are saying when we see firsthand, events such as climate shifts, that have changed weather patterns and continually destroy animals, people and settings with greater ferocity and repetitiveness? It was only a few years back when a certain Vice President lost the 2000 US Presidential Election and in so doing turned out to be the greatest thing that could have happened to the environmental movement. When Vice President Al Gore had the freedom to take all of his knowledge and life experience and present the decay of the world's environmental system in both scientific and common clarity, the environmental movement was finally defended by one of its greatest knights in shining armor. Of course there was no hill upon which to storm for the freedom of a country and the saving of a person from a tyrannical leader as is usually associated with great men of courage, but in this case he was able because of his STANDING in society, that's right because of his "Schmooze Factor" and connectedness in both political and cultural society to reach everyone everywhere. There was the added magic ingredient that I mention in STEP 8, he had been through hell in 2000 with his loss to George Bush Jr and the people saw him rise from the ashes. They felt for him and along with him realized that he was now embarking on the most important journey of his and our entire lives. You see this is the recipe for success.

His movie "The Inconvenient Truth" touched everyone. It made even the most apathetic of us all realize that something was critically wrong and that we cannot sit idle and not change our ways; if not for our sake then for our kids and grandchildren's sake. It was so powerful that even my grandmother who doesn't speak English knew who he was and what he was after. That is what your revolution/election or your vision/new reality (however you choose to look at it) needs to make it through the final hump.

So the question that is important now is who is your front page man/woman? Does he/she or you have a international, national, state or local power and influence? Does that person feel for the movement? Has he/she been personally affected or touched by this movement and do they have a story that people can relate to. If you look at past Presidents for example, you will realize that every truly great President had a way of connecting to the people. JFK was a World War 2 veteran, FDR gained firsthand insight into people's pain and suffering after becoming paralyzed and Lincoln felt that America was 1 nation and that once the Civil War was over, unified it would be an unstoppable powerhouse around the world. This must also be true for the potential office leader who is the go-to person for any big problem that no one else can solve, or the moms in so many households that can juggle a never ending list of chores without a second thought.

Basically, the same way big names get millions of people to movie theaters, you need those big names to help champion your cause as well.

In the case of political issues, get to know the players. Every time I speak with people that want to create change and ask them if they have taken their platform, signatures and documents to the elected officials, beginning at the local level, going upward to their congressman and state senator, I get what I call the "Confused Look", which of course makes no sense at all. How is it possible to change a law, which is of course the whole reason for a revolution if you never had any conversations or schmoozed with those who have the authority to enact the final change? What I mean is, you must be calling, scheduling meetings with actual agendas and taking minutes, speaking with others and asking to join their meetings with that particular politician.

Basically, I want you to be on his radar and for him or her to know exactly who you are and what you are after and if you are a nuisance to him, so be it! Did you really think you could make a change without being a pain! I don't think that's possible unless you already have access to powerful people and let's be honest this isn't the case for most people.

Now while you're in the "bothersome mode", for lack of better terms, ask what they are working on and which bills he/she is trying to champion. Perhaps you may be far apart on your issue and perfectly aligned in his other political platforms. If for some reason you have nothing in common with this person then you can always leverage your support including the extensive local contact listing complied through your work for your movement and aid in his/her upcoming campaign. This one will no doubt warm his or her heart and create a sense of camaraderie between the two of you. In the end it's all about trust, in politics especially, since your word means everything.

The strange part is, once you begin to speak with the mayor, the governor, the senator, his top aides, you get to know the crowd and begin to understand what works and what doesn't. Strangely enough, you may even begin to thoroughly enjoy the environment. Now before you start thinking that you have become a trader, you haven't, but the inner workings of government may now be, with your newfound understanding and appreciation, a future vehicle by which you and your movement may introduce and bring about change. You should be excited! Of course there is the possibility you feel the exact opposite and perhaps a newfound contempt for the system and its inner workings. Regardless of the case, keep your eye on the ball and remember, your group's revolution and the law that it will give birth to.

When people are working on the garnering support of influential people, they often assume that they need the big names that everyone knows; the Senators, the Hollywood elite or front page articles in the big daily newspapers. In fact what they actually need are those local heavy weights that can and will help you get the ball rolling. People like the head physician at the local hospital, or the Director at the biggest company in town, or maybe the President of the University or even the college head football coach. These are in fact the best people to ask because their support almost guarantees the support of thousands in their community. You must single out and quite literally have a working list of all these people in your town with "star status".

In addition, there may be times when all of your efforts may amount to nothing, it is possible and usually the more probable outcome. In these cases you may have to get down and dirty! No, nothing illegal, but I would think of creating another list but this time of those individuals in society that have always been on the outskirts of the status quo. What I mean is, do some research and find out who are these revolutionary warriors; whether they may be environmental activists or hard core political junkies for either party is irrelevant. Or perhaps they have been pushing for changes to the criminal code or maybe education reform. Regardless of their motives, these people are just like you! You are part of an elite group that sees the troubles of society and wants to do something about it, and your first job is to get others around you to realize what you have to say matters. The important thing to realize is that you shouldn't start from zero! Always leverage the "schmooze factor" in this step of the revolution as much as you can just like the big banks did prior to the crash of 2008 - I had to say it!

So what you have to do is make friends with the leaders of other movements otherwise known as Associations (by the way people are less scared by "Associations" than they are by "Movements" so keep the terminology in mind depending on the type of person you are speaking with). Ask other associations for their list so that you may contact them and provide your list as a way to help both movements. You may even decide to be part of their movement in an effort to meet others who are driven by change. Of course the people you court all depends on your target audience. You wouldn't court the minister of Justice if you were revolting against the government's cutback on subsidies to farmers. In that case the Minister of Agriculture would be your man or woman. But don't be fooled, if you somehow established a relationship with another high ranking Secretary or minister they would probably know each other leading the way for a very smooth introduction. Basically politics is more like a small town than a big city so watch what you do because in small towns good news travels fast and bad news at lightning speed!

Throughout this book, I have tried in every way possible to take a revolution and the corresponding election process and break it down to small chunks, 10-steps to be exact, that you can actually complete thereby increasing the momentum of the movement leading to its final success. Central to all of this work and analysis is the ability to answer the questions "What's in it for him?" and "What's in it for me?"

In the case of "What's in it for him?" you always have to have something that tantalizes them; something that interests them. The important thing is to never enter into a conversation or request where their support or approval is completely based on their MERCY. Nothing good can ever come out of this. Plus, if you don't have anything to offer, it could mean one of several possibilities; (1) that your revolution may not have the evidence to support your belief and that you may have to question your cause in the first place, (2) that you simply have to dig harder to discover the necessary evidence to better support your belief, (3) that you may be a terrible negotiator but still have a viable case, (4) that you are a terrible negotiator with a flawed case, or finally (5) that in comparison to other so-called major problems this one simply does not have the same importance.

There is another point of interest; they will probably ask "What's in it for you"? Now you have to realize that in a perfect world people do things for the greater good but in the real world, utopia is usually diluted with foul condiments. What I mean is,

The "Schmooze" Factor

some will take on different revolutions more for the impact a good fight will have on their careers than for the revolution itself which is fine as long as the movement profits from their work. What you may forget though, is that the person you are asking for support is quite interested in what you stand to gain personally, as well – a fact that is often overlooked from your end. This kind of understanding is crucial to your relationship with this person since the idea is that he/she will hopefully become your friend in the future, if you play your cards right!

These kind of friend/acquaintances are crucial because it equates to power by association. And in any revolution you need piles of this precious commodity.

Another error that most make in any movement for change is court those that already believe in them. Now I know it feels good to speak to an adoring crowd but a hard hitting speech to those who completely disagree is much better for the movement than you think. After all many of those people in that crowd may be torn and quite possibly are sympathizers or converts in transition. You need to attract these people any way you can because that is where the battle ground is set. Those hardcore believers will not switch from one camp to the other. But those uncertain of their position are up for grabs.

Let me ask you something, in your town, are people undecided regarding your movement? Do you even have the faintest idea except for the immediate crowd of friends and acquaintances as to the people's real beliefs? You see, people may believe in say the environment but if put up against their livelihood (ie their job), then your movement simply does not matter. You see this kind of information must be acquired to know where you stand. This is how you realize what people think, who thinks what and how much energy and effort it takes to convert people. By completing a door-to-door questionnaire with people, and retaining that information in a database, you will quickly be able to gage their attitude and after doing so throughout your community you will learn more about politics, salesmanship than you will have learned in any classroom.

Even more importantly, you will begin to learn what the "enemy" thinks. Why they think this way and what they use as their arguments to stop your movement in its tracks. You see these are the people that get you ready for debates because in their hallway, at their kitchen table, people reveal themselves and in general if you give a person the time to explain themselves without rushing them too much they will open up. People innately want to be heard and if you are willing to listen to them you will learn more than you ever believed you could.

Plus and this is the added bonus, when you speak to someone in their homes, they WILL REMEMBER YOU! In any election, people tend to remember and respect the person that presented themselves in person on their own time. They will quickly realize and sum up the kind of person you are and in the case of those who disagreed, well you just earned their respect and possibly their swing vote. Now say that at a certain point in the future you did decide to change things by throwing your hat into the political race for congress, those door to door discussions will become the support and hallmark of your campaign. And of course with the campaign comes the statewide audience and criticism that can take your movement all the way to law. Never forget every revolution, every movement and every election to legitimize the effort is nothing more than a huge group of people screaming and marching in the same direction in unison.

The one difference here is that in this case, if you made the right friends, joined forces with other revolutionaries, created relationships with the leaders of your community, and of course infiltrated the corridors of power represented via the attendance of the mayor, congressman and other member of city council those marches and protests have the best chances and the greatest hope for positive change - your change. I guess my only question is "How many people and influential characters have you schmoozed with today, yesterday and since the start of your movement". If you haven't, get started because your movement and advancement begins and ends with the schmooze factor!

Step 10

Race to the polls - Vote to legitimize YOUR revolutionary reform!

In this chapter you will learn:

- Forget the idea of "the old college try"
- "Judgment Day". - No election – No Reform
- Always, highlight your starting lineup
- Decide – Do I take my revolution to the next level?
- NEVER FORGET what the end product of a revolution is!

Step 10

Race to the polls - Vote to legitimize YOUR revolutionary reform!

This last chapter represents the final step in the "Election" Phase of YOUR overall revolution. This chapter marks the final and most critical piece of the puzzle because at this point you are on the verge of closing the loop that began way back in chapter 1 with the mind/heart/soul revelation for your cause.

I say this because it is at this point in time where people normally begin to tap themselves on the back and tell each other what good work they have done. They begin to recount and explain to any and all who will listen, of all the hours spent gathering people, drafting documents, creating certainty in their own hearts and minds as well as those of their fellow revolutionaries. Worst of all, even their speeches and discussions begin to be explained in the past tense, such as "the task had to have been taken on by someone, and we happened to find ourselves at the intersection of time and necessity". Like good students, they followed my ideas (consciously or subconsciously) on the importance of appealing to the crowds, diversifying the group and all of the other steps I explained throughout the book but they fell into the trap known as complacence and the inability to overcome the long and motionless plateau. The simple fact is, even though I agree that the work completed to date is commendable and you should be proud of it, YOU REALLY HAVEN'T DONE ANYTHING IF THERE ISN'T A SIGNED PIECE OF LEGISLATION THAT MAKES THE CHANGE CONCRETE AND IRREFUTABLE!

Basically what I'm trying to say is, "forget the idea of the old college try". It is better never to have tried at all, at least then you could have channeled all of your energy toward something you really wanted, achieved the goal you really cared for. Think about it, if the forefathers and the people of the American Revolution had given it the "old college try", the United States of America would never have been created. Imagine if they had prepared, marched and fought the English but in the end, didn't follow through because that last stretch was just too hard. The idea of the new republic would never have materialized. You see at the end of all the planning and fighting, what they ended up creating was some of the most beautiful pieces of legislation ever written; The Declaration of Independence and the Constitution.

These gentlemen didn't stand by in the late stages and let a few successful battles provide short term complacency that could have led to their downfall. They only celebrated once they had completed the mission; and it was considered complete only after the legal papers had been signed officially declaring the existence of the new republic, the United States of America; a country in charge of its own faith and destiny.

What I'm getting at is in fact quite simple. If your revolution happens to equate to a series of promotions to achieve your place as Vice President of Marketing at your company for example, you must not stop fighting your case until you have been awarded the title and compensation that goes with it. If you are fighting on behalf of environmental action, make sure your goal is properly defined and understood at the outset and then follow through with it until it has been achieved; I say this because in the environmental world, the goals are endless and so if still motivated after completing your goal then you can decide if you want to take on the next one at which point the procedure begins once again. Basically don't stop until the goal you defined in both documents, the SIMPLE VERSION AND ITS LEGAL EQUIVALENT ARE MET!

Now, having come to terms with the "old college try" factor it is in this step that you must leap over your last hurdle which amounts to the creation of a vote by your peers on the issue at hand. This vote means different things for different people – it can represent employee demand for the instating of a union to defend worker rights, a referendum on a particular state law, a vote amongst your group regarding the lead manager position for an upcoming project or a yearly vote regarding the rotation of the leader of your charitable organization. The examples can go on forever, but what I am getting at is simple – you must devise a process that will allow for change that is visible, fair, and acceptable to all. A process that upon completion, all involved will accept the decision rendered.

The degree of difficulty in the instating of such a process can range from simplistic to absolute insanity depending on the setting. The strange part is that when it comes to politics, this field is quite simple, in theory anyways, since regular scheduled election processes are fairly smooth and provide undeniable decisions (there are exceptions to every rule of course with the 2000 election being the perfect example). What I mean is, you have to lay out a procedure that includes the day, time and duration of the vote. How the votes will be counted (paper or computer kiosks), who will be doing the counting in the case of paper ballots, who will be overseeing the activities of the day, who will report the final decisions, and whether government officials should be present throughout the day in the case of non-government votes.

This may be a case where templates for voting processes can be acquired from unions and local governments as well as companies that have their own management/worker conferences without actual union involvement. These options represent some natural starting points with the best analogy coming from the military – agree on the "Rules of

Engagement" before you ever plan the date, time and the rest of the logistics related to the counting and processing of votes. The mere appearance of impropriety can ruin months and even years of work to arrive at this solemn moment in time.

In other words, Step 10 represents "Judgment Day" in the 10-Step Revolution process. The process demands that such a discreet point in time take place as soon as possible as this may be the first of many. It is at this or these points in time that the people in your district, fellow protestors, your boss at work, your fellow colleagues, fellow union delegates have their opportunity to vote and support or deny their approval for your ideas and leadership. Even more importantly, this action regardless of its result or magnitude must be recorded to show that the theory or the organization was tested in real life.

Furthermore, I think people are quick to assume that since you and your organization set up the vote that your point of view will automatically be implemented – Do not make this mistake as the vote tends to separate fact from fiction; what we believe is reality from what reality actually is and in so doing, provides the direction needed to legitimize the next set of actions or inaction depending on the outcome of the vote. Just as a side note, when you do ultimately achieve the goal or fail - it is always a possibility, and look back at the simplified Mission Statement written in laymen terms way back when, you will feel a sense of satisfaction and a belief in your abilities that no amount of money can buy, with the legal implications to prove it. Even if you brought it to the vote and lost the support of the people, this does not represent a loss. A loss would have been to stop the fight at anytime between step 1 and voting day. If the people disagree and vote against you, you won in the sense that you cleared the air and brought a new found clarity and assertiveness for what people actually think and believe and that is a win however you choose to look at it!

In addition to the notion of completion explained above, I highly suggest that throughout the fight and after the creation of the law, always ensure that you have highlighted those individuals that were instrumental to the success of the revolution. Don't repeat history on the grand or small scale by becoming one of those political tyrants who was overtaken by power's corruptive nature and the belief that it should all be consolidated in a single person - himself. This I would have to say is one of the greatest "human faults" that usually accompanies and destroys great military, environmental and social victories. Plus if you do decide to continue your fight to the next level then you will certainly have the respect and confidence of the "soldiers" that fought alongside you in the previous battle. Plus, this kind of PR gets around to many more groups and forums then you could ever imagine. Why do you think that a true revolution tends to include support from different groups all over the spectrum of the population? If you truly believe in the political push to ensure that the current President is a 1-term leader for example, then what stops you from requesting help through any of your lieutenants who fought with you during the previous environmental movement to champion this new fight? Nothing! They could represent the vital link to certain ethnic/religious/social groups of voters in your county, district or state? In other words, leverage the powers of your team members. Only when you learn to leverage will your ideas translate themselves into law!

This idea of leverage regarding laws has far reaching capabilities and powers. Furthermore, from a political point of view, I would advise that if a law was implemented at the local town or city level, it would be at this point that you would decide whether the fight should continue to higher levels of government including the state, national and even the international level. In other words, with a municipal bylaw in force for example, your message now has the stamina and more importantly the legitimacy to be brought to the next level.

On the other hand, and this is important to the resilience of the revolution, never be afraid to admit if you no longer have the time and the passion to champion and elevate the cause to the next level. This is not to say that you would undoubtedly be the best candidate to continue the fight but if you cannot devote yourself to the cause any longer due to other factors now taking precedence over the fight you have been waging, admit it and take the responsibility as leader to pass the baton to the next person in order for the next phase of the revolution and election to take place.

Lastly, you as the reader and as a present or future revolutionary must understand that society through all of its mediums will continually make the case for the link between the outcry for reform and the onset of anarchy, disorder and turmoil. In many ways, it's as though society at large, via all of its tentacles is disseminating propaganda that makes the case for a direct cause and effect link between revolution and anarchy. This is a dangerous concept especially since I have continually throughout this book repeated the praise, the mantra regarding the true goal of any revolution – The election of legal reform to benefit all of society. In this case society can represent any entity from your town, city, work place, or club all the way to the national and international arena. The crucial point is to judge a movement not by the chaos as portrayed by the media or certain groups but through the validity of the arguments and evidence as is hopefully described via the speeches and discussions of its leader.

What I am getting at then is quite simple. I want you to realize that revolutions against bad government, bad ideas is not anarchy! They are the calculated and carefully considered effect resulting from actions forced upon the people. Why do you think people campaign tirelessly to elect a new President every 4 years? It's because they have considered the arguments and results of the current President's time in office and disagree with his handling of certain situations. They then choose to revolt throughout the election so that change can be instated. This has all the hallmarks of freedom and liberty doesn't it? So then, what is so different if instead of a Presidential run, it is and environmental cause or perhaps healthcare reform or maybe immigration concerns. Whatever the case, all of these while being completely different are in fact quite similar.

In the end, what I ask is that you carefully consider all arguments before creating your revolution wherever and whenever it may be required. Using the steps summarized in this book, on my websites www.10steprevolution.com and www.silvioguadagnino.com and in my speeches and seminars, you can begin to carve out the form of your revolution and final election into law with the added comfort in knowing that it is anything but anarchy and actually one of the most powerful rights any person could ever ask for – the freedom and liberty to revolt against what we feel is wrong and then bring about the legislation to make the injustice a thing of the past.

The end product of a revolution is not anarchy, nor is it confusion or people chanting in the streets. It is the signing of the revolution into law AND NEVER FORGET THAT!

Conclusion

The intangibles

In this chapter you will learn:

- The intangible but concrete ideas
- You are now a creator; part of the "elite" club of those that help bring change to society!
- Help others tackle their revolutions
- Be vigilant – there are those who will stain your good name for their purposes
- If your vision became law – BEWARE – it is a living document and could die anytime

Conclusion

The Intangibles

In conclusion, I would like to close with a few suggestions, that I like to refer to as intangible but concrete ideas on what could take place in the near future if you decide to champion a revolution/vision and its corresponding election into law as explained via the 10-step process outlined in this book. Note these steps can be further dissected and analyzed in greater detail together at an upcoming seminar or coaching program with all the information available on my website www.silvioguadagnino.com.

Firstly your revolution is a creation, and whether you realize it or not every time you take up the fight for a cause you become part of an elite club that has existed since human kind took its first breath. You see, we who believe in change are always ready to accept or initiate it but it is, as you might expect, a lot more difficult than people realize. We creators/revolutionaries can envision the future and are not scared to leap forward into the unknown so that others can then follow and enjoy the new world or society that was forged out of thin air.

Apart from our renaissance personalities, that are deeply instilled in us all, there are a few actions that help us see our progress that most acknowledge, but very seldom practice. One of these invaluable activities is to keep a journal and always update it as soon as something of interest is learned, or an interesting fact or pattern is observed. It will be through this kind of record keeping that you will learn most about what to do, how and when to act and of course see unequivocally how you have grown during the process. Even more importantly, the thought process as described in your notes takes on a form that can be organized and reapplied in the future. There is only one catch here though - I have learned that if you procrastinate and wait till the next morning, or hour for that matter, to record the information you just learned, the information will be tainted, polluted and any other adjective you can think of that is synonymous with excrement! I am quite adamant about this because I have seen what resulted when I was meticulous in the exercise of recording of ideas for my own books, projects, as well as for work schemes with multinational companies and when I went at it freestyle; and the difference is unmistakable. Best of all this particular idea is true for anyone and everyone regardless of the work or activity you are concentrating on. So make sure you take those 15 min after a rally or an internal brainstorming meeting or discussion with a local heavyweight to write down a few notes as well as your hunches that came to you that very instant. Then top it off with the cherry on the Sunday; the action items that came to light and must be completed that will add momentum to your cause; Like I said a simple step, but one rarely taken seriously in the many failed revolutions of the past, present and future.

By the way, I know this is the modern age and everyone has the ability to say what they are doing every minute of the day, but in this case, keep these internal thoughts quiet and perhaps you can put it into your memoirs later on in life. You may even make more money that way! No one ever said a revolution can't be profitable, especially given the fact that all your work was pro bono from the very beginning.

Furthermore, there is a really strong possibility that you were helped by someone at the very beginning or at the very least, introduced to the idea for change by a teacher, colleague, friend or maybe even a complete stranger on the street. It is for this reason that it is your duty, whether you are successful or not in your revolution/election that you pass on the torch to another person or group of people, regardless of whether your revolution fazes out or keeps its flame burning. Who knows, maybe you are getting older and the person you teach ends up fighting for pension reform that provides you the security you need when you reach your golden years. The idea is simple "what goes around comes around", "energy is neither created nor destroyed just transferred from one form (or person) to another". Pick which ever slogan best suits you. Think about it, during the environmental movement of the early 80's when no one cared at all about the environment, if those people had not passed on their beliefs to new generations at a certain point the revolution would have died out. What happened was that those people infused the next generation which included family, friends but also strangers they met at town hall meetings or at their workplaces. The important idea to realize is that sometimes a revolution can occur and be confirmed in a relatively short time interval which includes the enforcement of legislation, but in most cases such as with the environmental movement, it is a never ending battle and therefore is always in need of being handed down from generation to generation.

While you can and should help those trying to get their revolutions off the ground floor, you must also be vigilant against all those who may want to use your good name in a revolution or idea that may tarnish all of your good work. This is a case where the tables have turned and you are now being targeted for help just as you were targeting others early on during your revolution. Now think back for a second at how devious you were in your thinking and thought processes when it came to acquiring the support of others? Now magnify that 10-fold because people and society tends to get more and more cutthroat with the years. The difference is that now you can really understand people's defensiveness and better respond to their requests having already stepped in their shoes.

This final point of interest is one to keep in mind as the years go by. For some revolutionaries your cause may have materialized into an actual piece of legislation, but despite this incredible achievement there is no reason that this same law could not be overturned, despite all of your work. You read correctly, your work could be completely overhauled to a shell of its former self or even overturned completely and replaced with the very ideas you fought to change. I think that this, amongst all scenarios, is the most difficult to digest because in this case, the reversion of the law comes slowly through an apparently harmless campaign to change the minds of the public, who over the years, changed their thought patterns and became "less naive".

I know this idea really does scare most people, especially if you were one of the revolutionaries that poured your heart out for the cause. Then again, you can rest comfortably knowing that this very fact unquestionably proves that democracy does exist, that it is alive and well and is forever changing.

Long live your cause, your vision and the 10-step Revolution that will help guide you towards its legitimacy and its conversion into law!

AUTHOR PAGE

Silvio Guadagnino began his career graduating from McGill University with a degree in Mechanical Engineering in 2002 and has worked as an engineer for over a decade building up experience in negation and project management for 3 Fortune 500 companies. It was throughout these 10 years that he realized how much he loved to write and inform people about his passions for politics, social issues, business, and most importantly how to attack specific problems facing people and society.

Silvio believes that theory has to be brought down to the level where it can be both entertaining and directly applicable to a person's life to create the desired outcome for the readers and listeners. He has presented his ideas to United Nations and government officials, to people on the streets, over the internet and to anyone who would care to listen.

He is also a private pilot, speaks 3 languages, has a business background in Stocks, Stock Options, and of course is a published author of this and other works. He believes strongly in people, their dreams and providing answers to the questions that matter most to them; especially to the ultimate questions that dictates our lives and ambitions ... Why and How?

Websites:
Central hub for links and information regarding Silvio's books, events, seminars, programs etc:
www.silvioguadagnino.com

The 10-step Revolution:
www.10steprevolution.com

The Means to a Chosen End:
www.chosenend.com

Seminars / Coaching / Speeches:
www.silvioguadagnino.com

LinkedIn
http://ca.linkedin.com/in/silvioguadagnino

www.ingramcontent.com/pod-product-compliance
Lightning Source LLC
Chambersburg PA
CBHW060535100426
42743CB00009B/1537

9780988020603